TRACKDAYS

The Glovebox Guide
Hamish Smart

The Crowood Press

First published in 2009 by
The Crowood Press Ltd
Ramsbury, Marlborough
Wiltshire SN8 2HR

www.crowood.com

British Library Cataloguing-in-Publication Data
A catalogue record for this book is available from the British Library.

ISBN 978 1 84797 111 1

Dedication
The hours, the work, the effort – everything that has gone into
making this manual a reality is dedicated to Mister D.

Acknowledgements
The assistance of the following in the preparation of this guide was gratefully received
and is acknowledged: Anglesey Circuit for access to the circuit for action photography;
Jonny Leroux at Bookatrack for access to a commercial track day for static photography;
Knockhill Circuit for access to the circuit for static photography; and Rob Price
and his magnificently presented Noble for assistance with action photography.

Typeset by Bookcraft, Stroud, Gloucestershire
Printed and bound in India by Replika Press

Contents

Preface

This *Glovebox Guide* is based on the ideas behind a proven instruction method. The basic premise is simply that you should throw the book into your glovebox and head for the circuit, using it more as a 'self-help' style of publication whenever you come across situations or problems during your day. If you want to learn by yourself, experiment, or you are unable to find the instructor on the day, just read the appropriate section whenever you would like some help.

It is not a substitute for the 'hands-on' type of instruction, but it will help you out – whatever your experience level – in a way that will allow you to strike a balance between learning and experimenting on your own, and getting that professional help from time to time to ensure that your skill base is being extended in the right direction at an appropriate pace.

The Guide is not designed to be the last word on the subject, or a book that attempts simply to teach you how to drive your chosen circuit, and for those reasons you will not find certain things in here. 'Oversteer' and 'understeer', amongst a great many other things, are defined in the glossary and mentioned only in passing. You need to know what they are, of course, but in this example, teaching 'feel' for such things and how to react to them (without a practical aspect) would be very difficult. Instead you will find handy sections, concise and clearly illustrated, that offer you answers to the questions that you may be asking, and hopefully you will find these helpful. Above all else though, the idea behind writing a manual that you can refer to throughout your day is to help you to think about the track experience and how to approach it, how to enjoy it more and, perhaps more importantly, how to improve each time.

Where problems arise or you find it difficult to advance certain aspects of your driving, you should have the tools to react to these problems, think about them, deal with them or try experimenting with certain driving components to alleviate them. If all you ever asked yourself during or after a track day was 'how do I go quicker than that?' then you are half way to the answer. As a result you will become a better track driver, more complete in your skill set and faster, smoother and more consistent in all that you do.

Introduction

Track days are now big business. Their popularity has exploded in recent years and with little wonder. The roads are more crowded and are littered with speed detection devices, making us all paranoid. Getting a thrill out of your own car is becoming more and more difficult. What is the point of having the performance without the ability to use it?

So, have you thought about track driving? It gives you the opportunity to take your own car to the circuit and explore a little more of its potential, and perhaps a little more of your own potential too. Alternatively, perhaps it will just afford you that one-off blast to blow away the cobwebs and revel again in the sheer enjoyment of just driving.

And why not? You can take anything to the track. That includes the car that you choose to drive, what modifications you have or have not made, what it looks like, the wheels and tyres you have – whether road tyres or track tyres – what it cost and a whole host of other factors. The cost of the car, the state of the paint or your bank balance genuinely do not matter.

From unmodified daily-drive road cars to track specials, genuinely anything will (or can be made to) go round the track with some sensible precautions. The only stipulation, of course, is that whatever you choose to drive should be exceptionally well maintained and *properly* roadworthy.

The track is a great place to explore any number of things – your own driving, your car's handling, any modifications that you have made since the last time you were there and driving at the limit – at speeds that today's speed-camera society will not allow you to do. Above all, it is a place to have fun.

Everyone goes to the track for their own reasons, but new boy or seasoned 'professional', you will find that a bit of fun is probably the underlying motive and, wherever you fit into the spectrum, there is a warmth and camaraderie that binds everyone together. (Seriously – just ask for the loan of a spanner, trolley jack, cable ties, hammer or whatever it is that you might need.) Everyone, whether quicker than you, slower than you, or even quicker than you think they should be, is there to enjoy themselves. Remember that you are at a non-competitive event though, and keep things in perspective.

Is the idea of track driving beginning to appeal to you? Consider these few words of caution before you get carried away: motor sport, no matter how uncompetitive it is meant to be, is (or at the very least can be) dangerous. It should be no more dangerous than driving on the road, and let's face

Perhaps more track-focused, this Noble is still a very capable road car.

it, no one sets off in their car intending to crash before getting the milk and papers in. However, there are always risks associated with driving, and there are risks involved in attending a track day just as there are when on the open highway.

There are a number of differences, of course. You might reasonably expect that higher speeds would be involved and that generally there should be fewer things to hit. However, although there are no cars coming the other way (perhaps a few facing the other way occasionally), you should keep in the back of your mind the fact that whilst there is no greater chance of an incident occurring, it can still happen.

Always try to be vigilant and conscious of your own limits. Do not get carried away in the joy of the moment and do not extend yourself beyond your comfort zone. This is very easy to overlook, so imagine what would happen if you crashed the car that you need to take you to work every day. As a general rule of thumb, if the answer is that you cannot afford to crash it, then you probably should not be taking it to the track. Thankfully, worst-case scenarios are very unlikely. Unlikely and impossible are, regrettably, not the same thing.

Once you have decided to do a track day and dip your toe in the water, what kind of preparation should you make, and what types of things should you bear in mind? What precautions should you take, what needs to be done to your car and what do you *need* to do or know? In short, where do you start? Well, *The Glovebox Guide* aims to give you some pointers to think about, starting from these questions through to completing a successful track outing, and ensuring that you enjoy yourself at the

Spare wheels, tools – what needs to be done to your car?

same time. It is designed to be relevant to anyone from any level, whether new to it all or seasoned track driver, as there is always something to learn. Importantly, there is enough information to get the novice started, and it is hoped that as your skills develop you can start thinking about your own performance, and that of your car, to see where you can try different things in order to improve.

1 Preparation

GETTING STARTED

Let us first consider practical issues. Initially, you must find out where any forthcoming days are going to be held. There is a guide to circuits and track day companies at the back of The Guide, so you should have a variety of choices. It might be sensible to pick a local circuit if this is your first outing, but there is nothing to stop you picking a track that is easy to get to, another track that you like the sound of, a track that you have heard is good or a track that suits for other reasons.

Above all, be realistic about the date you select. Check the calendar and compare that date with today. Is it far enough away that you can be sure that you have enough time to complete any preparation and purchase any items that you think may be expedient? Additionally, is there any

Do not let your brake pads get to this stage. These obviously need replacing, but check the discs very carefully too – they may be scored as a result of these pads disintegrating.

other foreseeable cirumstance that may prevent you from being there? Is your car due its MOT test before the day? Get it done before you book and pay – be sure. Do you know how thick your brake pads are, when the brake fluid was last purged, and how much wear is left on your tyres?

Track driving punishes these items (amongst others) much harder than road use, so you may have to think about changing tyres and pads beforehand. If you change pads, you may have to think about bedding them in.

If you elect not to change tyres, can you be certain that you have enough tread to get home if the day is either very dry, very hot, or both, as this may amount to something of a death sentence for most 'road only' tyres if they were marginal for tread in the first place (*see* top left photo overleaf).

You may care to plan ahead and buy some smaller containers of oil, clutch and brake fluid, fuel additive and so on, to take with you on the day. This is something that should be considered good practice. Constantly higher engine speeds can make any engine consume a little oil, so it is wise to take some with you and keep an eye on your oil levels during the day.

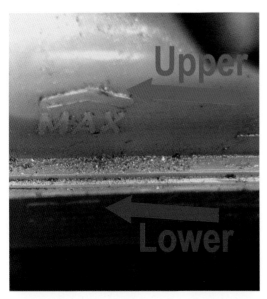

Upper

MAX

Lower

Good preparation – recently changed brake fluid. Nice and clear and topped to just below the upper mark.

This fast road tyre looks ready for another great day at the track, and it would certainly get you there... might not get you home again though!.

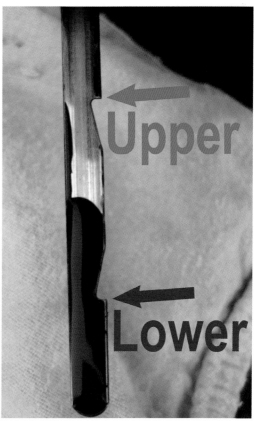

Although this oil looks quite old, there is still plenty of it. Caution is required with some cars vulnerable to oil starvation – the risk of damage can be reduced by running them full to the top mark.

Only 2mm left. Can you do the whole day and still legally get home again?

Even if you know the last time your brake fluid was changed, or bled, it is worth keeping a small container at your side. Brake wear is higher on circuits, as there is a huge difference between road driving and track driving. As the higher speeds reached on a track mean harder braking, this can generate temperatures that your brakes would not normally experience – in essence you can 'boil' your brakes far more easily on track. If in doubt, change the fluid before you go.

Depending on your mechanical skills you may also care to take a spare set of brake pads, or perhaps some other small mechanical components that you could replace easily should they be required. For some cars that have a known Achilles heel, taking replacements for those weak parts that are known to fail is also desirable. However, be realistic. If it is unlikely that you could replace them during the day then there is probably little point in taking them with you. A rally team can change a gearbox whilst the rest of us have a mug of tea, but mere mortals probably cannot!

The sort of rules applicable to brakes, tyres and so on can be applied to almost anything mechanical. If your car is making noises that you are fairly sure it should not be, it would be wise to get them attended to beforehand. Any noisy wheel or transmission bearings (typically a low rumbling noise), knocks from steering or suspension, squeaks from dry or ailing bushes, and any other bumps, thumps and rattles are, regrettably, not going to cure themselves.

The added stresses of higher-speed cornering, especially higher speed cornering allied to stickier track rubber, can see off bearings, for example, spectacularly quickly and in spectacular fashion if they are already failing. Think about the likely price of a mechanical failure on track! Even if you are lucky enough (or your reflexes are sharp enough) to prevent an incident, you may lose the entire day if anything fails first thing in the morning, and organizers are not going to be falling over themselves to give you any refund.

Think hard – make sure that everything is secure (especially the battery) and change whatever needs changing before you get there. That includes simple things like your wiper blades and the washer fluid. If you have concerns then book your car in to your trusted mechanic and get a quick inspection done – tell them why you are asking for an inspection and ask them to look out for things that may require attention, with reference to the higher loads that the car will be expected to cope with on the circuit.

In short – preparation is everything, so be totally objective. Consider whether what you have will offer you what you want when you get there, or whether some upgrades may be either desirable or an absolute requirement.

Old meets new, metal versus plastic, 20ltr each. Be wary, though, as some fuel stations will not authorize you to fill the plastic version unless it is appropriately stamped.

COST

Remember when costing out your day that the figure that the circuit or organizer charges is only a small part of the overall outlay. When you think about paying for the whole day, be objective about the overall costing, as you have to fuel up to get there and back, and your fuel consumption when you are actually on circuit will be much, much higher than you will ever experience in normal road driving. You may even need to think about fuel containers.

Think about any parts or repairs, and think about any overnight costs for accommodation, food and drink. Track days can be good value for what you can take from them, but few would describe them as cheap. Do at least consider what you will have to spend, when you will have to spend it, when payday is (if that is important) and any other cost influence that you think may be relevant.

Noise Restrictions

One really important issue that you should consider before you book any given day is the noise limit that the track you have chosen must comply with. Some are quite generous, whilst others, generally those tracks that are in the proximity of residential properties of some type, are restricted.

Cars with standard road silencing (with perhaps the obvious exception of TVRs and such like) will generally pass any noise limit check anywhere in the country without modification. However, if you have an aftermarket exhaust system or silencer, can you be sure that you will not be asked to go straight back home again having got to the circuit of your choice?

Some companies may rent you a noise meter, and you can buy them quite readily. Check your own noise output at the required revs and distance as, if you are at all concerned, it will be money well spent. Since there is no rule of thumb here, if in doubt, get it checked. You could ask your local MOT testing station as some, although they are likely to be few and far between, may carry the required equipment. If they do not, then they may be able to point you towards someone in the local area who does.

Advice and Research

Before you get to the track you may consider speaking to friends, colleagues, other club members, or even the people running the day (including instructors likely to be there) for any tips that they can offer you – and remember that anything born of experience is relevant.

Consume as much information as you can. If only the smallest amount of it is useful to you when you get there, then you will be better prepared, more knowledgeable, and perhaps as a result smoother or quicker when you drive – whatever your goal for the day. Do not act blindly though; if you have got some useful tips, think them through yourself, formulate your own opinion, and try out anything suggested carefully, just in case it works for someone else and their car and does not necessarily work for you.

Additionally, have a look at the internet (some useful web addresses can be found at the back of the book) to see if the circuit has a website with a track map. You may consider picking up one of the circuit guide publications for the track layout, and generally acquiring as much information as you can get your hands on before turning up at the circuit. Websites may offer other helpful items such as specific directions from major roads, and computer games can assist with rough layout, but all information is good information in this context.

If you can get to the circuit early (such as the night before) one of the most informative fact-finding missions that you can undertake is to walk the track itself – you can get a *real* feel for the layout, corners and bumps that you will be driving, and in particular things that you do not necessarily see or feel when you are 'busy' driving your car. It can be a fascinating insight in its own right.

Upgrades

You may care to upgrade some items on your car in advance of the day. This may be a personal choice, a result of the recommendation of your trusted mechanic, a result of research or a personal recommendation. Before you pitch in and buy some bits though, take a moment to consider your options.

First, do you really need some upgrades, want some upgrades or just think that upgrades are the thing to do? In some cases, for example if your brake pads are almost spent, then maybe this is the time to think about replacing your standard set with some more performance-oriented ones. However, if the pads are almost new, you may consider that now is not the time for this upgrade. Be wary, and always weigh the potential benefit against your own ability level. Novices will almost always benefit less from a greater performance

Perhaps close to the last word in upgrades, this original M3 may look standard. In reality it is only a paint job and some numbers away from being a race car for the road, but you do not have to go this far to have fun.

If you decide against any performance upgrades at this time, you could do a lot worse than invest in one of these.

level, and therefore you may be spending money that you do not need to.

That said, what upgrades could you consider? Well, perhaps the most obvious (and cost-effective) ones are brake parts, both pads and discs, then braided hoses and fluid. Indeed, there is a school of thought that says that if you are going to upgrade anything then brake products are where you should always start. Slowing down quicker is actually going faster after all! Stepping up the price spectrum, you could consider suspension parts, to include shock absorbers and springs, or perhaps tyres.

Most people will be aware of more performance-associated exhaust systems or back boxes, and freer flowing air filter cones but, as mentioned before, beware of increased noise from these items and view their purchase objectively before you take the plunge.

Perhaps even less common than these are things like more competition-focused seats and harnesses. These can be a benefit, and of course potentially offer a safety aspect too.

Naturally, modifying cars for track work can be a never-ending process, but there is time enough to match your ability level with new parts, wallet contents allowing!

Of course, you can do this on a budget, which was the message on the very first page of this guide; what you spend can be down to your ingenuity in sourcing whatever options you fancy; however, nobody will tell you that this is a cheap hobby!

INSURANCE AND RECOVERY

You may wish to consider insurance for the day. Are you insured for track driving? As track day activity is neither pace-making, competition nor rallying – which are often excluded from policies – some companies will offer cover for track days. However, this is becoming less common as more companies get wise to the increasing numbers of policyholders using the track as a vent and alternative to the risks they face on the public highways.

If you have a high-value car, or it is your only transport, or you are risk averse, then do consider getting the car insured for the day. There are some very reasonable rates out there, and although policies generally come with high excesses and exclusions for engine failures (for obvious reasons), they are still 'peace of mind' enhancers. If insurance will enable you to enjoy the day more, then it is obviously well worth it.

Recovery is perhaps well allied to the insurance aspect, and those more risk-averse may care to consider these items hand-in-hand. Should you

Insurance and recovery would be especially important if you were planning on taking in a foreign track. Always plan ahead when you are a good distance from home.

experience mechanical failure at the circuit, or perhaps fall foul of a more serious crash-based incident, what provisions do you have for getting your vehicle recovered and what restrictions might be placed upon this? Without wishing to appear overly cynical, it would be considered unlikely that your breakdown service are going to be enormously keen to attend your 'breakdown' within the confines of a circuit, particularly if your vehicle's breakdown has reduced its number of visible corners!

You need to be absolutely certain of where you stand before you attend the day. It is always worth phoning your recovery company and asking about their policy should you have any drama – perhaps you will be pleasantly surprised. Be prepared either way though, and you may rest easier throughout the day. This might be particularly important to you if you are a long distance from home.

If you find that you are not covered by your breakdown service, then be warned; recovery services are not cheap. It could easily cost several hundred pounds to move a car back to your trusted mechanic (or bodyshop) and there are circuits out there who are not keen on playing host to it whilst you sort out the logistics. Again, if you are risk-averse, spend a moment or two considering this before you attend – it could save you a bit of heartache.

When choosing a helmet, look for a sticker offering quality guarantees similar to this one – this helmet is approved for motorcycle racing

MAKE YOUR BOOKING

Be certain of all of the above – once you have satisfied yourself that all is well in the car department, that you have no commitments and you have a clear diary for the day itself, you are ready to book and pay your fee. You should note that this might be a deposit, which as with many things may be non-refundable.

Once you have booked you should get some indication from the organizer of how the day will be run, if you were not offered this information up front in the promotional material or on the web page. Will it be run in sessions, will it be 'open pit' (essentially meaning that you can come and go

as you please, although these are very occasionally limited to a certain number of cars if there should be a busy period), or will it be some other format? (*See* Appendix I for a sample of the sort of information that you might receive, and a couple of things that you might note as a result.)

If the day is to be run in sessions, how many sessions are you expecting? How many minutes each? Will there be a requirement for you to wear a helmet (most now do), and if so do you need your own? Will there be a stock to hire from at the circuit, and if so do you need to book this? Do think about whether or not you plan to do a few track days at this point. Everyone has probably been karting at some point and had to put his or her head into a sweaty helmet recently vacated by someone else – if this is likely to spoil your day, invest.

A good appropriate helmet should not cost you more than £100, and will last you for a good few years, providing that you do not drop it. The choice of full- or open-face is a personal one, although you may find full-face a better option if you have an open-top car, for obvious reasons!

INSTRUCTION

Whilst the section on upgrades talked about physical items, by far and away the cheapest additional performance you can buy is an instruction session. Whether this is a new track to you, or one that you are familiar with, consider booking some instruction so that you can 'fast-track' your first couple of sessions, get more familiar with the layout of the circuit, and perhaps take more from the day.

Even if you are familiar with the track, you may care to book an instructor. The many reasons for this could include a long break from track driving, a feeling of more confidence during the day should you iron out problems early, more speed if you can begin to understand the nuances of the track layout, amongst other things. If you think that you would benefit, then book – there is no cheaper 'horsepower' on the track than knowing where you are going and how fast you can get there early on.

Instructors are generally present at each day that you will attend, and are there to help you with anything that you wish assistance with. That sounds glib, but they will offer advice on anything from technical driving issues, line, marshals' post locations, rules for the day, and obviously all other aspects of your on-track performance.

Pricing varies, but the cost is never expensive relative to what you can take from a brief session. Remember that the performance improvement that you take from your session today should stay with you at every track you visit, and through each car you will ever own and take to any other track.

These two marshal posts, as you approach this fast blind corner, are important. Any incident on the other side of this corner can only be conveyed to you via the marshals and their flags, so a glance at the marshal posts as you approach this corner is extremely important.

Don't be shy about asking an instructor for help, and do not ever feel that the instructor will be sitting in your passenger seat thinking that you are an idiot, or that he will be observing you in any way other than objectively. Everyone has to start somewhere, the instructor has seen it all before several times, and unless you genuinely are behaving like an idiot, he is not there to judge you. Since it is you that has asked for help, he is there to make sure that you take the most from your day, hopefully go a bit quicker and all in total safety.

Helmet and Clothing

For the day, you may well be asked to ensure that your arms and legs are totally covered. This is not to ensure that the marshals do not have to look at a variety of uncommonly white limbs, but to protect from any glass cuts if you crash or have a windscreen fracture and blow-in.

Make sure that you are wearing clothes that you are comfortable in, and are preferably not too heavy (as you will conceivably get quite hot, particularly in race-style seats), but above all else make sure that there is precious little of 'you' visible to the outside world. If you have a full-face helmet, you may care to consider that having the visor down will improve protection should you

Appropriate gloves make a lot of sense for track work – choose from leather-palmed (on right) and suede-palmed.

Slim-soled trainers make ideal track driving shoes, but you could invest a little more in some racing/karting style boots. Both are lightweight and offer great pedal feel.

have an incident, although it is recognized that this may not suit everyone.

Footwear is probably the most important component of the average person's track attire, and you should think about this carefully. Clearly, turning up in jackboots is neither necessary nor really desirable, and ideally some thin-soled shoes or trainers would be better – it gives you more feel and, obviously, the less weight that you have to move when you move your feet, the more agility you will have should you need to react to something quickly.

Some people buy lightweight race/karting/climbing style boots, but before rushing out to follow suit, ask yourself if you really need these items first. There are other purchases that will probably offer you a greater value return to your basic performance, particularly if you are either new to, or inexperienced in, track driving.

Lastly, gloves are a very wise purchase for the track. Appropriate gloves will eliminate in one strike any incidences of sweaty palms giving you grip problems, particularly if the weather is hot, or you have an old, and well-polished, steering wheel. As they are relatively inexpensive, they are well worth considering.

TYRES

Tyres are your lifeline and sole contact with the tarmac that you will be running on. For this reason, it pays to consider what you have fitted presently and what you can expect from them.

Budget tyres are cheap for a reason. If these are what you have fitted to your road car, then by all means run them on track, but you may experience lower levels of outright grip, particularly if the day is wet (or greasy), as they tend to be turned from harder rubber. For the novice, however, perhaps this offer of a lower level of outright performance could be considered an advantage, as they will tend to keep absolute limits lower. Drive with this in mind and you will have just as much fun as anyone else.

Road tyres will offer perfectly adequate grip levels and progressive handling on the circuit. Most cars would have been fitted with these when they were new and, albeit designed with road noise constraints and a decent lifespan in mind, they will be good in all weather conditions.

Keep an eye on your treads though, as extremely hot days will hurt them, taking the edges off the tread blocks, and consequently reducing outright grip. As with any other type of tyre, watch your tread depth like a hawk – you are expecting to drive home on them.

Fast road tyres are likely to be a softer tyre than the road tyres mentioned. It follows that grip will likely be better (probably in all conditions) but lifespan will be shorter. These tyres are perfectly useable for both road and track and, although likely to be a bit more expensive, they might be a natural progression for you if you have not yet found that second set of wheels and the extra down the back of the sofa for the ultimate tyre.

There are several tiers of performance all the way through to the 'dedicated' track tyres which are rather impractical for road use, although in some cases not illegal, but offer stunning levels of grip on a dry track. These tyres are more slick-surfaced in nature, have stiffer sidewalls and squarer shoulders for better cornering grip. They are going to be expensive, but the rewards for the more experienced driver can be worth it.

This section is really here for illustration only, and in no way should you rush out and make purchases of any of these items without considering whether or not they are suitable for your own requirements. You can turn up and drive with whatever you have fitted from wherever on the tyre spectrum. You should, however, always be mindful of the fact that a more worn tyre, or perhaps a budget tyre will offer lower levels of outright grip, and your driving and expectation should accommodate this.

From left to right, dedicated track tyre, fast road tyre and regular road tyre, some rather more worn than others! Note that there is more rubber in contact with the road on the track tyre than on the 'fast road', and more on the 'fast road' than on the regular road tyre.

Dedicated track tyre, although not illegal for road use. Not cheap, but with precious little in the way of water drainage, and softer rubber means huge grip and huge grin!

Road tyre – well-defined tread blocks and large drainage channels for versatility in all weathers and a decent lifespan.

A lot of people are using a second (dedicated) set of track wheels and tyres these days. This represents a good way of making sure that your 'road' tyres are always going to be legal for the drive home. Good practice, if you do have a second set of wheels and tyres, is to roll each tyre the whole way around its circumference both before fitting and after removing from the car – it gives you a great chance to check for damage or defects, uneven wear and feathering (the removal of slivers of rubber from either side of the tread edge) of the tyre.

As the tyre is your contact with the tarmac, and the source of your traction and grip, it will pay you to know that each time you take to the track your tyres are set to the correct pressure (do it before you get there) and in the best possible condition, something that you can then take confidence from when pressing that little bit harder.

If you are swapping wheels over it is good practice to also check your road set fully when they come off and before they go back on too. A further benefit of swapping wheels over is that it enables you to clean brake dust off both sets easily and before it sticks properly. Because it will!

It goes without saying that should you find defects, then it is not worth taking the chance – the tyres are your lifeline so you cannot afford to

One of the newer generation of fast road and track tyres – no real definition in tread blocks, but with squarer shoulders and with some water drainage channels. More rubber on the tarmac means more grip!

Pencil style tyre pressure gauge – accurate and easy to use. Simply press on to the valve, allow the slide to register pressure, remove and…

…read the pressure off. 31psi. Perfect!

compromise for the want of saving a few pounds. Replace them whenever it is necessary!

There are two additional items that are relevant to this section. The first of which may seem like a strange link, but it is worth mentioning fuel canisters. If you are running on a second wheel set with track tyres today, and fuel is not available at the circuit, it may not be practical to change your tyres simply to drive to the fuel station.

Fuel canisters may, therefore, be a subsidiary issue to 'track-oriented' tyres, but if you have such tyres you may require to take fuel with you. Make sure that you think about the requirements of the day as there are few more irritating things than a perfectly good day run short for the want of some more fuel.

Pressures for your tyres on track are a black art, and will naturally differ from car to car, tyre to tyre, day to day, track to track, and depend largely on weather and temperature. The hotter tyre temperature, through the extra effort and load, means that the air inside will expand, increasing pressure.

A little rise in pressure is therefore expected, and you could, if you feel confident, drop back a couple of pounds to standard road pressures. Although, if you are running on a sessioned day where your next lap may be the best part of an hour away you should be wary, as when you next venture out on to the tarmac your tyres will be both cold and under pressure. If you are inclined to experiment, then go right ahead, but each time you venture back out on to the circuit you should be very cautious. You should also ask yourself whether you have attained a level of ability where tyre pressures should be your focus rather than other aspects of your overall performance.

PASSENGERS

Doubtless at some stage you will wish to take your friends, family, girlfriend, boyfriend or whoever out for some laps in your car. This is absolutely fine, but remember that they are in your car, and you are in charge. If you require anything specific of them, do not be afraid to ask. You do not need distractions, so make sure that there will be none whilst out on the circuit.

Some common-sense things to ask are that they do not speak to you when you are concentrating, that they simply turn off their mobile phone and that they comply with any other small request that you may have. Even if it is simply that they fasten their helmet or do their belts properly, you should ask – remember that it is you that is in charge, your car and your responsibility.

If you have harnesses fitted, and you are taking a passenger out during a session, make sure that you have satisfied yourself that they are properly strapped into them. Many people will never have come across harnesses before and may not understand how to set them so that they are secure. (*See* Appendix III.) It will sound a bit daft as without doubt you know how to make yourself comfortable in your own harness, but you should make sure that you understand how to strap someone in yourself in case your passenger is perhaps having some difficulty.

Remember that harnesses are probably no better than seat belts if set incorrectly, and they are certainly more uncomfortable under larger cornering and braking forces if they allow just a little movement!

Never allow the simple presence of passengers to distract you from driving your own laps. Keep your focus, and do whatever you would have done without them there. If you feel that having a passenger at this time will make you less able to concentrate, then do not be shy about telling potential passengers that you would like to do this (or any) session on your own either. Whether this is simply to facilitate better concentration, or where you do not feel comfortable with someone alongside you, do not be bashful – just be polite, and hopefully people will understand. It is important that you are focused and comfortable,

in whatever sense, and that you can concentrate fully.

Finally, always confirm with your organizer that it will be acceptable to take your children out in the car with you.

VIDEO

By all means video your laps from either inside or outside the car, but, as with passengers, *never* play to the video camera either. Remain focused on your own job, do whatever you would have done without the camera present, and do not extend yourself simply to 'catch that moment'. There is absolutely no kudos to be found in video footage of your own crash.

It is worth noting that most circuits and organizers will now require any video cameras to be hard mounted, and not held by passengers. Some will not permit their use at all.

This simple looking bit of metal mounted securely to the rear shelf makes a very effective (and compliant) camera mount.

2 On the Day

ARRIVING AT THE CIRCUIT

If there are prescribed items that you must have with you on the day, then lay them out the night before at the latest. Some circuits or organizers will demand that you bring your driving licence, whilst others require the MOT certificate for your car. Use the prompt of getting these things ready beforehand to have a think about what else you might choose to take with you.

Good practice is certainly to have a few odds and ends, perhaps like a small tin of WD40, some cable ties, basic spanners, screwdrivers, sockets and pliers. Additionally, you could quite reasonably include a torque wrench, tyre pressure gauge, tyre inflator, tyre tread depth gauge, a spare alternator belt or any other thing that you think might prove useful.

It is track morning and you have arrived. There may be a tendency to let the excitement of the occasion run away with you, so even if you do feel excited about the day, it is worth slowing yourself

DRIVERS SIGNING ON

Some organizers and circuits may help you out with locating 'sign on' – the briefing may be in the same place.

down a little and attempting to remain calm about what lies ahead.

Do not drink coffee or energy drinks before the day begins as you do not want to be excessively jumpy and you do need to concentrate – only the

A selection of items from the boot – trolley jack, axle stands, fuel, oil, coolant, penetrating oil, some tools and the all-important cable ties! Missing from the picture are items including a torque wrench, the wheel bolts to replace the locknuts, vinyl gloves, and a spare set of brake pads. Take whatever you think may prove useful.

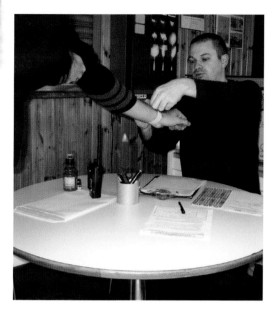

Some organizers may issue your wristband directly to your wrist – this is for obvious reasons!

most tardy of people will find that the adrenalin of the track does not wake them up properly.

As a prelude, try to ensure a good night's sleep, and if you need to be there early, give yourself plenty of opportunity to do so. Do not leave 'just enough time', as that will not allow for a traffic jam, puncture or any other eventuality en route. You should aim to be there in good time in order that you can change any parts you intend to change, check all of your important levels, present your car for scrutineering (where applicable), noise testing (where applicable) and any other requirements as laid down in your information pack for the day.

You need to clear all of the rubbish from your car (and that means everything – no steering lock bars, nuts, bolts, brackets or bottles of water should be left in the cabin whilst on track), *and* still make 'sign on' and the briefing on time, preferably all without rushing.

Sign yourself in, sign your passengers in too, carefully affix any identifying stickers to your car in the prescribed places and any wristbands to yourself.

SCRUTINEERING AND NOISE TESTING

Scrutineering is not part of every track day that you will attend and, where it is involved at the circuit, there can be different levels and different forms of inspection.

Some organizers do not inspect your car at all, so the onus is on you to ensure that everything is in proper order. Some organizers will ask that you 'self-scrutineer'. This is a form-based scrutineering, whereby in filling in the form you are certifying that you have checked your car over and everything is in order. This normally consists of a tick-box style form with questions as to certain aspects of your car: wheels, exhaust, oil leaks, steering, battery and bodywork to give a few examples of items that you may be asked to comment on, or certify that they are in order.

Alternatively, you may be formally scrutineered by some organizers. This will involve a suitably qualified person looking over your car to ensure that you are presenting a properly track-worthy car.

The one item that the scrutineer will almost certainly look at is the security of your battery and its terminals, and they will then go through their own checklist for your car. Perhaps on the list will be your fuel system, exhaust, engine fluid leaks,

Battery security is important – this one is going nowhere from under this substantial metal retainer!

You may be issued with a sticker for passing scrutineering, noise testing or even for attending the briefing.

Conventional auxiliary bonnet fastening – the scrutineer may be interested in the security of your body panels.

bodywork and bonnet fixings and security, down to the mount for your camera and so on.

The list will be varied, but you must pass on all counts. You will nearly always be allowed to present your car again if you fail on anything, so do not panic if you fail first time.

Likewise, noise testing is not necessarily a part of every day that you will attend, but on a 'noise limited' day you will be asked to present your car for noise testing. This involves holding your engine at either a preset rev figure or percentage of maximum revs with the noise tester placed a specific distance and angle from your tailpipe to take a reading.

Be aware that this procedure does not sound particularly mechanically sympathetic, but you will have to endure it to get on track.

If you are given a sticker to indicate that you have passed scrutineering or noise testing be diligent about affixing it to your car where indicated.

If instructions are given as to where to affix these stickers be diligent about this. If no instructions are given then adopt a common-sense approach keeping them away from your line of sight, and beyond the sweep of your wipers too.

BRIEFING

Listen carefully to the briefing – it is not because someone likes to be the centre of attention that they take the time to talk to you before going on track. Nowadays there are legal obligations in a briefing, as well as an informal sort of roll call, and the body of the briefing will offer many useful snippets of information to keep you right through-out the day.

This may include the format of the day and any changes to it, a rundown of marshals' flags and what to do when you see them (or see them removed). Sometimes the location of marshals' posts may be included (and that includes the end of the pit-lane and what you are required to do or show there), as may any further special instructions that you should know about. Some are track-specific so do not assume that you have heard it all before – you almost invariably have not. In particular, know when you are supposed to be in the paddock, pits or assembly area if you are running in a sessioned day – there are no refunds for missing a session.

In addition, you should know when you are meeting with the instructor if you have booked a session. Make sure that if instructions are given as to where to meet, that you are there too and that you are ready and clear as to what you would like from the session (if you know) so that you can explain this to him.

Most briefings should offer you the chance to ask questions, and if you have any then do not be bashful. The organizers will be happy to answer anything that you can throw at them. Some offer

Briefing is a formal event, but often has an informal feel. Here you will get comprehensive information and instructions to make sure that you get the most from your day.

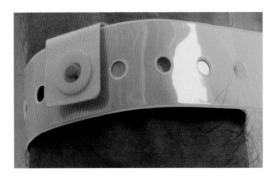

Affix these plastic bands securely and comfortably – you will probably be required to show this to the marshal allowing you onto the circuit from the pit-lane.

additional useful tips such as the location of the nearest petrol station, to very specific information about where water gathers on a wet track to bumps and ripples that you should watch out for. Be certain to have all your information requirements satisfied before you step into the car.

You may be issued with a wristband or sticker to prove that you have been in the briefing. Again, be diligent about affixing stickers where indicated. If you are given the plastic sort of wristband make sure that it is fixed properly and is not uncomfortable.

THROUGHOUT THE DAY

Even the most experienced driver will attempt to start the day slowly. There are a couple of good reasons for this. First, you will get a good feel for the track, the car, the weather, and your track mates in this session, so make sure to be observant and try to garner as much information as you can. Second, it will (hopefully) enable you to calm yourself a little, and in a more calm frame of mind you are less likely to make mistakes, more likely to be observant and more likely to set yourself up for a slow build-up during the day, rather than trying to do it all at once.

There is no glory in spinning during the first session, and on some days with some operators this

may be considered a first warning in a potentially very short day should you do it again. Be warned.

The rest of the day should be a progression. You should always be aiming to improve on each session, and you should be building up towards the end of the day, when you should have your best session. There are, however, a couple of provisos here. Should you feel that you have reached your peak earlier than the end of the day, do one of two things.

First, aim for a consistent approach to each subsequent lap – do not attempt to increase speed or alter line. Just make sure that you hit the marks each lap and aim for laps that are mirror images of each other. This can actually make you slightly faster as you free up a little brain time as the approach to the consistent lap starts to become more second nature. Be vigilant though – if you make several small errors or feel that this is not working for you at this time, make yourself take a short break, or a longer break if you think that you will benefit from it.

Second, if you are happy that you have done all you came to do, or you feel that making small errors is an indication of fatigue, why not leave it at that? It is a lot cheaper to stop early than it is to repair a damaged car, so don't chase the ghost – a lap or time (note that track days are not competitive events in any case, and that timing is strictly prohibited under most operating companies' public liability insurance small-print) or particular corner, particular speed or line that is not there. Never try too hard.

Endeavour to learn and progress your skills, but try to do so in a measured fashion, perhaps slowly if that suits your learning style. If you have already achieved all that looks possible from the day, try to recognize this. Relax and have some fun – these days are all about fun. You could ask someone for a passenger ride or simply pass the time chatting – whatever appeals to you once you have parked your own car.

There is no need to make sure that you drive every minute that you are entitled to – apart from anything else, your car may not thank you for it. Do not worry about having paid for track time not

Passenger rides are commonplace at the track day. The camaraderie and warmth of reception are such that most people will happily take you out in their car. Just ask!

used, as it is still cheaper to 'lose' £40 or £100 than it is to fix something that you did not need to break, and in any event there is no glory in damaging your car *just* to get an extra session, five minutes or whatever timeframe.

In short, take it easy; give yourself and the car a good cool down before either calling it a day or having another go. If you have had a good day, then stop and have a chat, relax, but above all remember that you have enjoyed, and are still enjoying, yourself.

It is not by accident that track days are deemed not competitive, timing is prohibited and (for want of better words) contact discouraged. These rules are there, some for obvious reasons, some not, but they are a sort of informal rein to keep everyone minded of their own limits and the random elements that driving amongst (potentially) many other cars can introduce. The rules are

a good way of keeping a lid on potential ego problems and over-enthusiasm, and are no bad thing. In view of this, do try to pay attention to your own levels of fatigue and concentration, particularly on open session days, where you can conceivably be out on the track for prolonged periods of time.

Do not allow yourself to be distracted by any thoughts not relevant to what you are doing – do not react to poor driving by others or people waving at you from the pit-wall or taking pictures of you as you go round, to give a couple of possible examples.

If you feel that you are not as focused as you should be, or you notice that you have made a small error or a number of small errors in a short period of time, then you may be fatigued, and perhaps coming in and taking a break is a good idea.

Remember, however, that it is not necessary to take a break after making an error. If you are quite confident that you know why something happened, then this would be another example of something that you should not dwell on and become distracted by. Focus on not letting it happen again, rather than the fact that it just has.

It is worth thinking about what you wish to achieve when you are at the track too. As mentioned above, people turn up at the track for a variety of reasons, so it is worth casting a thought in the general direction of your motivation for being there. If it is simply to have some fun, then great, but you will have a lot of fun getting the basics right in any event.

If you wish to achieve something additional, what is it that motivates you? What do you want to achieve – are you interested in advancing your general trackcraft abilities, or would you prefer to concentrate on certain aspects? Perhaps you want to improve your braking, cornering speed, turn-in, observation, confidence, car control (at whatever level), timing (and this means the timing of certain things such as, for example, your re-application of the throttle in the cornering sequence, rather than the timing of laps) or some other facet of driving on the track.

There are many trackcraft abilities and all are valuable in putting together a complete package of skills, making you a more complete driver. You can concentrate on one or more elements as you feel able, but an instructor may be the best way of highlighting the way forward in each case.

Think about booking that session, as you can make a huge advance in one session if you are clear about what you require, the instructor is clear too, and you are prepared to listen and act on his advice. The instructor will wish to help you so there is no point in paying for his services if you are not prepared (or able) to take his pointers on board.

Lastly it is very important that you keep a good focus and attitude throughout the day. Driving on the roads these days can be frustrating and this might be why you are at the track today – there are just so many 'idiots' out there, right? Remember that we all perceive things differently, and therefore your definition of stupidity may not be the same as someone else's.

On track, you will come across people who are learning and make silly mistakes, and those who are experienced and still make the occasional silly mistake, and those who are inexperienced or genuinely nervous about taking their road car out on the track. In short, you may come across those whom you might define as 'idiots' on the track too. The difference is that on track you have to ignore them, be patient and not let them get under your skin. Remain totally focused on your own job whilst driving. **Do not** let yourself become angry or frustrated at another's actions, as you cannot afford to divert your attention. Stay calm, take whatever action is required and then get on with your own lap.

If you really have a grievance with a fellow driver, make a quiet mental note and then speak to the organizer, marshal, steward or instructor when you have parked your car in the paddock and taken a moment to compose yourself. They will take matters from there.

3 Pre-Lap Checks

BASIC CHECKS

Levels   You will have had a good check around the car before bringing it to the circuit, but it remains good practice to check your levels before venturing on to the track each time. Your car may use more oil running hotter and at higher revs than on the road, and that in itself is worth checking.

The upper and lower marks are clearly visible on this clutch reservoir, but where is the fluid? The level can be seen right at the bottom of the container, and this clearly requires some investigation.

Since it is possible that coolant will also run hotter, this is worth checking too, as are the levels in your various reservoirs – brake, power steering and clutch (if you have a hydraulic clutch) to make sure that there is no significant difference from before. Note that a real difference in either brake or clutch fluid levels may mean that your brakes or clutch have become more worn and this may require attention.

Fuel   There are a couple of facets to this section. Naturally you should always cast a glance to your fuel gauge before venturing on to the circuit. This is good practice in any event.

If you have noted that you need some more fuel then, clearly, you have two choices. The first is to venture from the circuit to the nearest fuel station selling your required fuel type. Alternatively, you may have planned to bring fuel with you in appropriate containers, and if that is the case then you can simply fuel as required.

However, and as referred to earlier, worth thinking about are the options you have if you have arrived at the circuit and changed on to your track set of wheels. Leaving the circuit may no longer be a practical suggestion as your tyres may be inappropriate or even unsuitable for road use. You may have to think about whether or not changing the wheels over is an option, and if not then perhaps get containers enough to bring fuel for the whole day. Or find some very obliging friends or fellow track-dayers to help you out perhaps!

Brake Pads   You will have checked your car over before bringing it to the circuit, but there are a few things that are worth checking again before you start each session. Brakes handle a greater work-load on the track, and your pads will wear significantly quicker here than on the road.

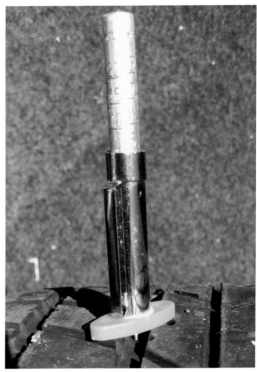

The brake pads are not easy to check with the very restricted view through the wheel – be diligent about checking them, taking the wheel off if you have any concerns.

Checking tread depth is really simple with this little gadget. Extend the pin then press onto the tyre face and…

Have a quick look through the wheels and verify that there is a good amount of pad left before you start the session. A slightly softer pedal in a session may indicate that the pads are low, so a quick look may save you some grief and embarrassment in the next.

Tyres You will also have had a look at your tyres before the event, and it remains good practice to keep an eye on these throughout the day. You must always be mindful of the fact that you may have to drive home on them at the end of the day, although this aside you should always be checking for damage or uneven wear patterns.

Moving tyres around simply to even up wear side-to-side, or front-to-rear where appropriate, is good practice on road tyres. Remember to leave that all-important 1.6mm of tread to make sure that you can get home legally.

Wheel Bolts There are two issues to be mindful of in this section. First, wheel bolts get very hot as a result of dissipating braking heat, and although it stands to reason that they start off cold, and should cool down again, this hot/cold cycle means that it is good practice to check the torque settings of your bolts before you head back out on to track again.

If you do not have an appropriate torque wrench to hand, a check that they are every bit as tight as you set them before you went out previously will suffice. Remember that this is particularly good practice if you have changed to 'track wheels' after arriving at the circuit.

The second issue here is that whilst a lot of track users doubtless will have locking wheel nuts or bolts in place, it is very good practice to remove these before track work, replacing them

The torque wrench is set by turning the metal collar. Dial in your car's required setting – here it is set to 101lb ft

...read the measurement off the cylinder. The lowest complete sector gives you your measurement, so here the tyre has about 4mm of tread left – fine for going home on!

with additional standard 'hex' wheel nuts or bolts.

The hot/cold cycle is the principle behind this good practice, and whilst it is nearly always possible to remove a standard hex pattern retainer, irrespective of how seized it has become, the more complicated (and sometimes fragile) nature of the locking retainer means that they can be very difficult to remove if seized. Rather than take the chance, replace the locking nuts beforehand – it may save you great difficulty when you next require to change a wheel.

Bonnet Pins   Before you head out on to the track, if you have bonnet pins and these are the type that actually lock (i.e. with a key), make sure that you have them set to the unlocked position. In the event of any under-bonnet drama, marshals may

Tighten and then torque your wheelnuts according to this numbered sequence. Remember to remove the locknut (shown at position 3) beforehand though.

It is good practice to remove the locknut, so note the four regular 'hex' nuts on this wheel. The numbers shown display the tightening sequence for four-stud wheels.

This is a fixed towing eye on an older vehicle. Modern cars generally have removable ones, and it is good practice even if not a briefing requirement to have it fitted before your session.

not have the time to ask you for the key, and you may not have the time to unlock them. Without wishing to make this sound too melodramatic, if you have any engine fire issues, your bonnet may be very hot and getting this open (or off) quickly is a priority.

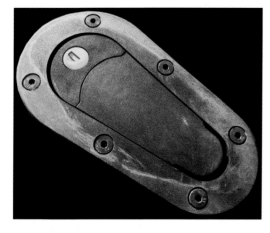

Neat fitting bonnet catches like this can be locked closed. Ensure that you unlock them before venturing trackward.

That said, do make sure that these are secure before you venture on to the track, particularly if these are the only method by which your bonnet is secured. Verify that they are unlikely to be affected by the greater speeds on track.

Towing Eye If you have a removable towing eye, as most modern cars (with plastic bumpers) do, you may have been asked in the briefing to ensure that this is both fitted and its position is obvious. This is to make things easier for the marshals should you find yourself in the unfortunate position of requiring a quick recovery.

However, it is good practice, even if this is not a briefing requirement on the day, to fit your towing eye anyway. Should it be required, you can take the pressure off those attempting to help you, and since you may already be stressed a little in this position, having one less thing to worry about is one less thing to worry about!

Common Sense Turn off your radio and mobile phone before you venture out onto the circuit, and with the latter (amongst other items) make sure that it is stowed properly. You do not really need any further distractions on circuit, particularly something as avoidable as a phone ringing or items dislodging and moving around you in the car.

SEAT, MIRRORS AND CONTROLS

Ensure you cover the basics first, so make sure to get your seat comfortable.

First, a general but almost universal point, you should be sitting further forward than you do when driving the car on the road. A good guide to where is, with your back fully against the seat, loosely to drop one arm onto the steering wheel. Letting your arm go floppy, at the least your entire hand should be in front of the wheel (on the windscreen side) with your wrist now resting on the steering wheel top. Of course you can be closer than this if you find it comfortable and doing so does not impair your range of movement.

Any further back than that, and it is actually more difficult than you would think to have total freedom of your arms' sphere of movement without moving your torso in the seat. A better level (and ease) of control is the motivating factor here as, if you get into trouble, you should be reacting with fluid steering inputs, and not having to move your body in order to make those movements – you may not have the time, and if you are harnessed in you may not be able to!

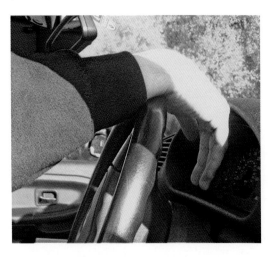

Sit a little further forward than you likely would for the road. Getting your wrist on top of the wheel like this indicates that you are seated about right!

Second, make sure that once you have moved the seat to enable the above, you still have complete freedom to move your feet accurately around the pedal area.

Third, make sure that you have reset the mirrors so that you can see all around you from this revised seating position.

One of the most important things that you should remember before setting off is the position of your hands. Place them on the wheel at either 'quarter to three' or 'ten to two' and then leave them there.

Do not shuffle the wheel, irrespective of what your driving instructor would have to say about it. Once your hands are on the wheel you have only the one reason to move them – your left hand (assuming a right-hand drive car) is required to change gear, but that should be the only time that you are not gripping the wheel.

Once the gear is selected, replace your hand. The wheel is your link not only with the immediate direction of the car, but to control and communication from the tyres about available grip. You cannot do anything more important with your hands than keep them stapled to the wheel!

Grip the wheel firmly and ensure that you do so throughout the day, but do not be fooled into gripping the wheel too tightly, as some novices do, as it does not necessarily follow that a tighter grip is a better grip.

With regard to seats, mirrors and controls, before you set off from the assembly area, try to set two things firmly in your mind. It is very common to see novices (and even people who have some experience) constantly looking in the mirrors to the detriment of their own driving.

In the briefing the steward, clerk or event organizer will likely have offered advice on where overtaking will be acceptable and likely as not on which side this will take place. This information will prove very useful throughout the day – once out on the track, by all means be aware of the traffic around you, whether in front or behind, but as overtaking may only be permitted in certain areas, do not obsess on your mirrors if you are not in one of those areas.

Be polite though, and should you be able to let someone through safely (and 'safely' should be emphasized) in the areas where overtaking is allowed, then you should do so.

SETTLE YOURSELF DOWN

A good rule of thumb, although one that some people do find difficult to follow, particularly novices, is that you should always try to be as relaxed as you can be.

If you are a little excitable when lining up in the paddock, there are a couple of useful 'tricks' that can help you out when taking to the track. It sounds like a potential penance, but these can be very effective tools to steady your nerves, settle into the job at hand, and ensure that your day gets off with the best possible grounding on which you may build.

You could try setting yourself a voluntary rev limit. It could simply be knocking a thousand or so off the actual limit, or it could be any other number that you choose. The idea here is manifold, but for the novice it serves to try to reduce the adrenalin rush created by that acceleration buzz and the higher engine revs in your ears. This serves to try to eliminate things that you would probably not find desirable in the first couple of sessions. This is

particularly true if you are finding yourself jumpy or nervous.

Another useful exercise for the first couple of sessions of the day can be to select a single gear in which your car can pull the whole lap (or very nearly the whole lap if you find a track with a particularly tight hair pin, for example). That gear will most likely be third, although this is a short track technique, and you may find it inappropriate for anything with really big straights. That said, where you can work it, it simply eliminates a distraction, particularly if it is either a new track or car that you are experiencing for the first or second time.

Remember to blend out of the throttle in really quick sections of the track, and try to really smooth out the corners to get the best idea of line and speed. Learn the layout and corner approach in a controlled basic build-up, and once you have mastered the layout and corner speeds you can take control of the gears again.

Take control of the gears again as soon as you feel ready, but do a good few laps without them if you feel that it is helping. Equally, take control of the gears again quickly if you feel that you already have enough confidence and focus to cope with all the things that could be new to you at this time.

Try these if you are prone to over-enthusiasm, whether the result of nerves or not. They are not for everyone but they do work.

The hair pin at Croft is one of the tightest corners that you are likely to drive. You may have to drop a gear here if you are attempting to drive that disciplined 'third gear' lap; you may have to move one hand off the wheel to get a little more steering lock too!

4 Warming Up

SIGHTING LAPS

It is time for the first session of the day. There are a couple of things that you should think about here before you start. A common format these days is for a pace car to go out and lead your first few laps round slowly. Use this informal instruction session wisely. On your first lap of the track look out for the marshals' posts, any cones laid out for you, and other visual clues that may prove useful.

This gravel is easy to see off line with a camera, but not so easy from your seat at speed. Try to use the warm up laps to observe anything likely to influence your lines and grip later on.

More useful than at roadworks, you will likely see a few cones like these placed at key points (brake, turn-in, apex and exit) round the track.

Cast a frequent eye over your gauges frequently to ensure that everything is fine, and try to get a feel for the conditions on the tarmac surface, with particular reference to the traction, grip and braking performance that you may expect when you begin to get up to speed.

Look particularly for changes in surface, debris (stones, for example), rough areas to avoid, shiny areas to avoid, kerbs, white lines and areas where tramlining (where the car wanders through compressions in the road, and steering to get the car out of them can be quite difficult) may occur – in short try to map the rough layout of the circuit in your head.

Remember that different surfaces offer different grip levels, and although not exclusively, white lines, particularly when wet, offer precious little, old tarmac will offer some, and new tarmac will potentially offer lots of grip. Use this information later when you are getting up to speed.

If you are a new driver (either generally or just to this circuit) it is well worth trying to get to the assembly area early, so that you can be out behind that pace car – further back in the queue, the appropriate line can be relayed in a sort of 'Chinese whispers' fashion, and can be some distance from the actual (and proper) line. If you are unable to get right behind the pace car, and find yourself several cars back in a sighting lap queue, then try to be objective about following the car in front, as they are likely to be following the car in front of them.

If the line is not obvious to you, then you have a couple of laps here which offer you the ideal opportunity to experiment (at a lower speed) with several different lines – the smoothest is likely to be right.

It is important to note that if you genuinely cannot find something that works, or more likely nothing that feels right, ask for advice from an instructor or trusted fellow track-dayer to help you out. You will get far more from this than simply pressing on yourself and getting yourself frustrated if things do not come to you naturally. Do not be shy about asking for advice – everyone has at some stage!

If this is a new circuit to you then add the physical layout and direction to your observations too – try to assess corner radius, length of straight, and perhaps a likely line that will suit your own car and driving style.

If you have previously 'driven' the circuit on a computer game, then be realistic about the physical differences that you can see and use the drive round to add 'body' to the electronic information you have already garnered. It is a great way to learn, but must be treated with some caution, particularly with specific circuits.

Ease yourself into the day, even if you are a seasoned regular, as it will be to your advantage to check that everything is working, and that you are happy with it. Remember never to mistreat a cold engine – take it easy, drive your own laps and build your own speed and comfort margins throughout the day.

Build engine revs rather than using them all at once, or even set yourself a temperature (on gauge or dial) before which you will be taking it easy (or easier).

When the green flag is waved, signalling the end of these controlled laps, do not treat or interpret that as a sort of carte blanche – still build yourself in gently, smoothly and gradually, as this will assist with your day, whilst not asking too much of your car all at once.

Note the pit-lane exit line – when leaving the pits take care to stay inside it. When on track take even more care to stay outside it – the speed difference could be quite large between you and someone joining the circuit.

An oil pressure gauge is a better benchmark than a coolant temperature gauge. Oil takes longer to heat initially than coolant, so if the pressure is still quite high at idle, take it easy until the oil warms and thins.

You are also likely to find out the easy way if anything should go wrong once the car is loaded up and approaching track speed, although hopefully your preparation has eliminated all but the tiniest chances of this happening. Above all else, never overstep the mark at which you feel comfortable, irrespective of outside forces, such as cars that you think that you should be faster than, or overly enthusiastic passengers in particular.

BE CONSISTENT, SMOOTH AND CONSISTENTLY SMOOTH

'Smooth' – this is probably the most important watchword in the construction of the perfect lap. Smoothness of input applies to every major control in your car, and every movement you ask of each of these controls. The concept of maintaining smoothness of input is key to the stability of the car through any portion of the track, and the stability of the car is the key to the speed that you can carry through any portion of the track.

You should always be smooth with steering inputs. The more fluid your instruction to the front wheels, the more chance they have of being able to respond and do what you ask of them if they are reacting to smaller input force changes.

When making a turn, feed in your steering input smoothly and gradually and you will not overwhelm the available grip of the front tyres. Your input does not need to be fed in slowly, but unhurried commands should make for quicker and more accurate progress.

This approach holds good for braking too, as the more smoothly you brake, the more slowly the front of the car loads up with braking force; in short the slower and more smoothly weight transfers to the front of the car. This allows the tyres a more gradual build-up of braking force to deal with, and means that there is more chance of slowing the car whilst remaining in full control.

When you release the brake, however, the opposite occurs and rearward weight transfer attempts to rebalance the car. The more smoothly you release the brake, the less tendency there is for the front tyres to become 'unloaded', which may cause instability, particularly in lower gears or tighter turns.

The application of the throttle is the same too, and also creates weight transfer, particularly where you have a good amount of grip (and/or a lot of horsepower); the more smoothly you apply the throttle the more chance there is that the driven wheels can cope with the increase in forces being asked of them, resulting in more acceleration than simply planting your foot on the floor in one action.

Conversely, removing your foot from the accelerator (particularly in smaller gears) creates weight transfer too, so lifting your foot smoothly (albeit quickly, just not suddenly) creates less forward weight transfer, which could unload the rear wheels and cause instability on turn in to, say, a quick corner.

The concept of smoothness at the controls applies to any major control that you have at your disposal, so not only steering, brakes and throttle, but gear selection too. Be firm and positive, but smooth too with both clutch and gearlever - the less rushed the better, and the less chance you

No instability here in this very fast right-hander!

have of instability created by the gear coming in with a 'bang' as the clutch is re-engaged.

What about 'consistency' then? Consistency is mentioned elsewhere in this guide as the ideal focus – an approach if you like – where you cannot see the next step up or improvement on any given day. It can be a focus in its own right though, and you do not need to wait until you reach an impasse on the day before making consistency a priority.

In this context, consistency is the key to making your approach to your lap more second nature.

If each lap round you are able to maintain an ideal line and good speed, being as smooth as you can, then each further lap round you are reinforcing that approach, that line and that speed.

The more that this happens, the more this becomes a slightly subconscious process, a more second-nature process, and this then leaves you more processing time to work out the next small improvement, negotiate the next obstacle or solve the next issue needing your attention.

5 The Lap

COMPONENT PARTS OF THE LAP

You can break any lap down into component parts, all of which are the same lap after lap, on any circuit. You can also break the component parts down into smaller parts, which again should be the same lap after lap, circuit after circuit. By focusing on each element, you can build up the armoury of track elements that you can cope with, and this in itself will give you an idea of your strengths, and perhaps weaknesses too. However, to illustrate this point, let's look at the complete lap in component form. Every lap on every circuit

Oil Temp

Oil works very hard on track, so if you have an auxiliary oil temperature or pressure gauge fitted, do pay particular attention to both.

will follow this template. It might sound slightly oversimplified, a bit daft even, but every lap has a number of corners and a number of straight bits, and that is it.

Straight bits and corners. Nothing else. The straight bits offer precious little challenge – anyone can drive fast in a straight line. Perhaps the only few things that you might want to do on the straight bits are wander from left to right, or vice versa, to line up for the next corner, have a small rest, relax your hands or feet, and you should certainly take a split second to check your instruments and mirrors, perhaps allowing faster cars past.

In broad terms (note that there are, of course, exceptions), you do not have to worry too much about the straight bits, other than where they begin or end, but what about the corners? The corners are the features that define your lap, and for each corner there are a number of elements that follow sequentially for each corner of each lap of each track.

The thread that binds these elements defines the approach that is required, so it is the link between the components of each corner that we are about to look at.

THE RACING LINE

What is the racing line? The fastest way round a corner is not the shortest (running round the inside of the kerbing), so try to think of driving through a corner rather than round it. How do you do that? The short answer is the racing line. Confused?

The racing line is the fastest way round the circuit, but how it relates to the tarmac on which you drive is perhaps more complicated to explain, and establishing exactly what is the fastest way

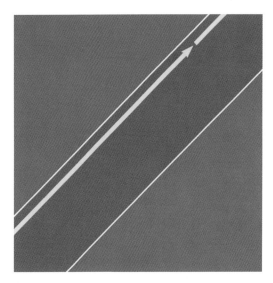

The racing line on a straight section of track is simply a straight line.

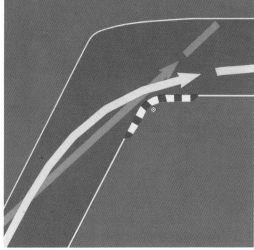

With this sharper corner, the orange line shows that the racing line is not a straight line. The yellow line suggests the quickest path, the racing line!

round the circuit can take some time, even if you have some experience. The easiest way to illustrate the point may be to have a look at the following four diagrams.

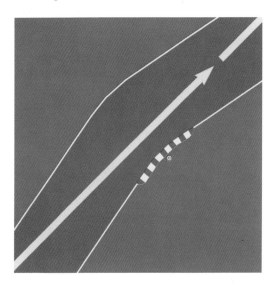

Due to the gentle nature of the bend, there is no need to deviate from your course and the racing line remains a straight line.

In the first diagram there is little doubt about the quickest route through this section of track. No corner means no braking and no steering. The racing line here is exactly that – a line.

In the second diagram (bottom left) there is a kink in this section of track, and if taken in isolation (meaning that we ignore what came before this section and we ignore what will follow) then the quickest route through this section is still clear. There is a straight path through the centre of the kink, so there is still no need for braking and no need for steering. The racing line here is still exactly that – a straight line, taking the shortest route and passing the cone at the apex.

In the third diagram there is a tighter corner than in the second diagram , and on this occasion the orange line shows what might happen even where it was possible to start to the extreme left of the track. There is no straight route through this corner as that line illustrates – it falls short of being able to get all the way through without deviating.

For this corner there has to be steering input (and there may have to be braking input). The yellow line, illustrating the racing line in this case, shows the shortest and fastest route through the

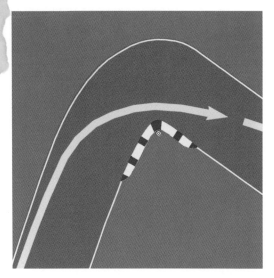

This severe bend requires much more steering input. However, it is important to note that the racing line is more gentle than the corner itself.

corner, just missing the apex cone and deviating as little as possible from the straight line.

By deviating as little as possible from the straight line, as shown in the first two diagrams, it is clear that, for this section of circuit, less speed requires to be sacrificed yet little steering input is required. The racing line is a gentle curve, and it is worth noting that the curve is less than the curve of the corner itself.

The fourth diagram shows what happens when the corner radius tightens further. In this case there is no question of that straight-line option, and steering input is required. (Braking input is also almost certainly required.) Again though, the principle is the same: to minimize steering input, to minimize speed loss and to minimize the deviation required from the straight line. The racing line here is a greater arc through the corner than in the third diagram , passing the cone at the apex, but is still significantly more gentle than the severity of the corner.

Since we have established that the racing line is the fastest way round the whole circuit, we can conclude that maximizing the speed through corners, by straightening them as much as possible,

adds to your lap. Getting it right is immensely satisfying, and by getting it right in the corners, you have a better chance of maximizing speed down any straights – the less turn involved, the earlier the possible application of throttle when coming out of a given corner.

Naturally, using the racing line makes you a smoother driver, a faster driver, a better driver, and it should follow that the smaller and smoother inputs make you a safer driver too, since your car is being asked to react to less.

Essentially then, this smoothest and fastest line is the racing line. The racing line uses the smallest steering input required for the corner, the least deceleration, the earliest acceleration, asks the least of the car for the given corner and maximizes road use. In short, it is the most efficient way of getting the car through the corner and on to the next straight.

There are exceptions to this, such as complex or sequential corners (*see* photo overleaf). Additionally, there are variations to the type of apex you may encounter. There are early apex and late apex corners, and these also require little variations (turning earlier or turning later) in approach – ask the instructor to help you with a given corner where the line feels alien or difficult to find. He will be able to help.

Anyone can drive quickly in a straight line, and the corners are the features that define your lap, so now that the racing line is a little more familiar, let's break the corner down.

CORNERING

1.   Thinking Point   There is a conscious moment before physical inputs start – before you have done anything you should already have thought about the corner itself. How tight is the corner, what camber (if any) does it have?

You should have decided where you are going to brake, which gear you know will be the most appropriate, where you intend to turn in, or what visual clues you will be using to determine where that is. You will also have decided where the

This complex sequence means that the first corner (the left-hander) has compromised line and speed as a result of the slower right-hander (in the foreground) to follow.

apex point you wish to use is – remember some, if not all, circuits lay out cones for you to use as pointers, so if you intend to use them, you should remember to think about them and focus on them throughout the cornering sequence. You should have dialled in enough thinking time so that you can get through each point in the sequence with all aspects of previous points completed.

It is sometimes also a useful approach to adopt a sort of 'plan b' mentality – what happens if something unexpected happens, or if the sequence changes for some reason? What would be your approach if, say, you observe a slower car that you are almost certain to catch mid-corner?

Where external influences of any type arise, have you enough time and processing power to select an alternative? In short, try to be proactive about such things where you can. Think about it, as it could save you from any number of unfavourable outcomes.

Dial yourself in a second or a half second more than you think that you will need to get the car stabilized and ready for the turn – you would be amazed what you can do with a spare second.

Once you are more confident and comfortable, and you have achieved more consistency, you can reduce this additional thinking time – indeed you may even find that you remove it almost automatically, and that your options sort of announce themselves to you, almost subconsciously.

2. Braking Point Some tracks have markers laid out for the novice driver. Even if you are not a novice, you may do well to use these markers to start your day. Naturally, they are set for a reason, but equally naturally not every car and driver combination would require to brake at that exact point. Use them as reference pointers, but consider using them nonetheless.

Once you have assessed what happens when you brake at these markers, you should always feel free to adjust if necessary, but you should not feel obliged to change simply for change's sake. If you feel comfortable with the markers, then great, as that is one less thing to concern yourself with straight away, and you can get straight on with a sort of 'join the dots' approach to learning the line, as that is what the cones or markers represent.

The mighty Eau Rouge at Spa. If ever a corner was likely to get you thinking about your approach, it would be this one.

What is the braking point, and what should your actions be at this point? It sounds simple – it is the point at which you apply the brake to set your speed for the forthcoming corner. This is certainly true, but it dramatically oversimplifies the thought process and the actions themselves.

Initially, there is the actual point at which you start braking. That may be at the marker, it may be slightly after the marker; it may even be slightly after/before whatever marker you used last lap if you are trying to find a better one.

Then there is the action of braking – is a light brush of the brake required to scrub a little speed for a fast sweeper, or is it a hair pin bend? How hard and long you brake for will be determined by the approach speed and the target speed – what you are trying to remove is the gap between these two speeds, but there are many ways to achieve this reduction.

Ideally, you want to leave the braking zone in a stable car, so you may brake harder to begin with than towards the end of the braking zone to ensure less weight transfer as you approach the turn-in point.

How it is achieved is very much a matter of feel, and some will tend to use constant brake pressure, with others modulating brake pressure. The target speed remains the same so the net effect has to be the same, but you can dramatically prejudice the car's stability into the turn-in point by trail braking (still braking as you turn) or by reverse weight transfer (essentially the car's weight returning to the rear as you release the brake) as you turn.

To ensure that you get all of this right, it is worth braking earlier at the beginning of the session, then reducing the braking distance whilst increasing the braking effort until you are satisfied that you have got the best 'distance/stability on turn' combination.

If you struggle with this, and many do, get an instructor to assess your braking performance – it is very easy with minimum effort to increase your performance in this respect, and a trained eye should spot any potential problem areas and potential improvements very quickly.

Naturally, there may be the requirement to change gear as part of this slowing down

41

Fairly unambiguous instruction here, but this is the marker for the circuit's own race school and may not suit you. It is a great place to start though, and you can hopefully brake later as you get more confidence.

exercise. Gear selection, although it contributes to retardation effort, is a separate function (not intrinsically, but physically) and is treated as such in section 12 a little later on.

It is accepted that you might find that no braking is required at all, and perhaps just a 'confidence lift' is the order of the day in, for example, a fast sweeper. Then, and bearing strongly in mind vehicle stability, this section of the sequence may be bypassed, and you would lift and reapply throttle as detailed in the next section.

3. Throttle Adjustment In the preceding section, stability when you reach the corner is mentioned more than once. The combination of the most fluent line and the most stable car round any given corner gives the best corner speed and, therefore, the best speed into the next aspect of the track. This is particularly so if you have a straight following the corner.

The line, commonly referred to as the 'racing line', revolves around linking turn-in point, apex and exit point, but the stability is created when the car is being asked to perform as few separate tasks as possible at the same time. To assist with this, once braking is complete and the target speed has been attained, the throttle should be pressed to create a stable car – what this means is that the car should not be being asked to accelerate (positive throttle), and nor should it be being allowed to decelerate (negative throttle).

The throttle should be approximately neutral, with just enough energy being asked of the engine to maintain the car's speed through from the turn-in point to the apex, and perhaps beyond.

Remember that in turning the car, some speed is being scrubbed off through the simple act of making the car deviate from the line it was previously running along, so the throttle may require to be ever so slightly positively pressed to maintain speed.

This will largely depend on your car, so try simply maintaining the speed through the corner to start with, and if you need to apply a bit more throttle then do so. You should be trying to do

Pre turn-in; braking done, gear selected and neutral throttle equals stable car. Bring on the corner.

this by ear or feel though – there is no excuse for looking at your speedometer whilst trying to take a corner, and no good reason for doing so!

4. Turn-In Point The same applies here as did to braking points, as a lot of tracks will have a marker for you to use, helping you to turn in at the appropriate point. Do make use of this marker, as likely as not it is the one that they lay out for their own race school, so it will be in the 'ball park.

You should not, however, feel bad about adjusting it a little either way if you find that you get a better line and feel from doing so. If you find that you have moved your turn-in marker a lot to either side, perhaps think about this again. There is a reasonable chance that you are doing something wrong – you may consider moving back to the marker and starting again.

What do we do at the turn-in point? Well, it would be easy to assume that all you have to do here is make the car move into the corner, towards the apex and on through to the exit marker. That in essence is correct, but you will have to read the radius (the tightness of the corner) and work out how much steering input will be required. That in itself is really only the start of the process though.

Remembering the 'smoothness' message from earlier, you would hope to make a single smooth turn of the wheel, all the way from your commencement steering angle to the steering angle that you will need.

Making one turn helps with the stability of the car through the initial turn process, gives the steering tyres time to bite and make the car alter its course, whilst not rushing the input ensures that there is time for you to confirm to yourself that you have got it right and make any corrections that you may require. This approach also gives the tyres the smallest force changes to deal with whilst still getting the job done.

At the turn-in marker, so make that turn! Remember to turn smoothly and progressively keeping stability and speed.

At the turn-in cone, ready to make the turn. Turn and…

Any corrections that you have to make are fine – don't feel bad about them. If you find that you are making a number of adjustments, however, try slowing your corners down until you get more comfortable, reducing adjustments in the process. Then you can build back up again.

You should remember that with this topic there might be a compromise – how about, for example, multiple corners, or if you have just overtaken another car? You may find yourself 'off line' or not where you would ideally choose to be if you are in a sequence of linked corners.

In this position, things can get tricky, so you should apply all of the rules above, but make your initial approach (and actions) for the 'entry' to the next corner based on where you find yourself now. You may have to consider compromises in terms of speed, track position, braking effort, line, steering input, entry, apex and exit points and so on – virtually every part of the corner can be altered if you are off line or in the middle of a complex sequence.

Be patient, and apply the appropriate rules to each part of the corner. Remember to begin slowly and build up, and on the first couple of laps ensure that you have enough time to establish what elements you need to think about. Then, and it sounds obvious, think about them. If you have

to slow down even more, do so; consider it part of the learning process, but never feel bad about it.

If you are still having difficulty, and this is quite possible as even advanced drivers can struggle with complex (or linked) corners, slow the corner sequence down to better understand the facets, come off track and have a think about it in a more settled environment, or perhaps enlist the help of the instructor. He knows what is required, and should be able to iron out any problems with haste and minimum fuss.

A last word here is that after you have passed the turn-in point and hopefully completed all of the actions that you need to, you should move your gaze to the apex. The human brain has a happy knack of helping you to get to where you are looking, a useful fact to bear in mind when at any part of the sequence.

5. Throttle Adjustment   Once you have the car turned and you are heading for the apex, you might find that in open, or opening, corners or perhaps more likely in corners with late apexes, you can start to apply throttle almost immediately.

Of course, you would have to assess the corner itself and the amount of grip available to you when working out how much throttle you can use, but it is possible to get back into the throttle very early in such circumstances.

…look at the apex cone to help guide the car there.

When assessing the corner itself, you should make certain that application of the throttle is not going to prejudice the stability of the car or give you issues with running out of track to the outside, but where these are unlikely to happen, then you should certainly feel very able to add some more speed.

6. Apex The apex is the point of the corner where you should have your car closest to the inside of the bend, and may be denoted by a further coloured cone at most tracks. Your turn-in and throttle modulation in the previous steps should have enabled you to position the car at the apex, exactly where you wanted it to be.

The car should be stable through the apex. This stability should give you the best possible mid-corner speed. Mid-corner stability will give the best possible platform for getting the car cleanly out of the corner and on to the next visual clue (the exit point) and next action (more throttle, corner allowing, less perhaps if you are running out of road!).

When leaving the apex point, you should already be looking at the exit marker. This has advantages as noted above, as the brain will allow you to follow your gaze, guiding you towards it. It has the further benefit of offering you the chance to look through and out of the corner, and down

In this shot the camera is sited at the apex cone. Already past the turn-in cone (in left of shot), the driver is looking for and turning towards the apex cone.

Reaching the apex with the car still stable. Good speed, good line. Spot on so far!

the next portion of track, should visibility allow. You can then decide on the throttle required for that bit of tarmac.

7. Throttle Adjustment At the apex you should be able to assess whether or not you can accelerate towards the exit marker. If the road is opening up in front of you and you have enough tarmac to play with, then increase the throttle.

Remembering the smoothness mantra from earlier, you should attempt to blend from your current throttle position to the target throttle position, full throttle if you can see that you have the opportunity. If it helps you to modulate throttle use, count yourself into the pedal. It need not be long – one or two seconds from no throttle to full throttle is enough, and helps reduce the forces acting on the driven wheels.

This maintains stability, reduces wheelspin (or the tendency to actual carspin if you are rear-wheel driven) and gives you the opportunity to wind off

steering lock (if you are able to) towards the exit point. As a general rule of thumb, although not totally exclusive, you can be adding more throttle as you are removing steering lock.

8. Exit Point This is the point on the track where, having crossed to the inside of the corner for the apex, you return to the outside of the track, thus ensuring that you have created that perfect arc (the racing line) through the corner.

The exit is often marked on the track for you, perhaps by a further cone, and this should give you an indication of where you are supposed to be when leaving the central part of the corner. Although perhaps the least critical of the markers, there are some obvious reasons why you should still try to end up there anyway. Perhaps the most obvious reason, is that it is the line used by the track's own racing school or professional instructor for training purposes, and is perhaps therefore the ideal marker for the corner. The exit point is also

Now past the apex and the road is opening out – perhaps wind off some steering lock and apply some more throttle?

Now at the exit of this right hand corner, and the road has opened up but is still gently turning right. Add some throttle? Of course, as this is a fast section of the track, but hang on to a little right-hand lock, and remember to balance the two to retain stability.

on the track, and you really want to be on the track. Additionally, it may be a guide to things that you cannot see, and may not be able to determine. For example in complex or sequential corners, it may tell you where you should be on track and may not therefore be an obvious exit marker for the corner that you are in if taken in isolation.

Think about it – albeit perhaps the least critical marker, if you are missing it by 'miles' each time then there is something wrong. Ask the instructor to help you understand why you are missing it and that should help you move back to a more realistic exit from the corner.

Be objective here though, and do not lose heart, as there is one potentially huge positive to be taken from this – if you are not getting too close to the exit marker, this might mean that you could be going faster!

Remember that when you are at the exit point you should still have the car stable and (where there is no other corner in the sequence) be on the throttle in order to propel yourself down the next portion of the track. You should already have assessed that part of the track and should already know what is waiting for you there, both in terms of additional traffic, corners or other hazards.

Where the track that follows is both straight and an allowable overtaking spot (perhaps as per the briefing information) you should not be so rushed that you cannot make a quick judgement call via your mirrors to assess whether or not you should be blending out of the throttle slightly to allow faster traffic to pass, or perhaps assessing a

car in front for a passing manoeuvre yourself. The briefing will have advised what you need to know and do for either scenario so now follow those rules carefully.

9. Throttle Adjustment This item is here because, in certain corners, you may have to wait until the exit marker before being able to adjust the throttle. Should this be the case, for example in complex corners or sequences of corners, or perhaps even just tighter corners, simply follow through the rules in the above section, just a little later.

Again consider that the car can only deal with a finite number of forces, and where you are able to wind off steering lock, you may be able to apply more throttle, balancing the total of these forces, whilst still maintaining stability.

10. Visual Keys At each point on the track where you have to take some action, it is helpful to have visual clues as to where you take those actions. At various points above, we have looked at the fact that most circuits now leave cones out at brake, turn-in, apex and exit points, or some combination of these. However, as also discussed, these are guides and perhaps not the definitive marker for you and your car.

If you find that the markers are not right for your car or pace, you need to find some other way of gauging where to brake, turn-in and perform other track actions. Try looking for advertising hoardings, tarmac join lines, plants or shrubs, a mark on the kerbing or even a portion of kerbing (for example, the third red section, or fifth white

Spoilt for choice approaching this braking marker, there is a tarmac join, a white line, a cone and dotted white line further on, the cabins, plus the taper of the banking and barrier right, and different colours of barrier left.

section, or whatever happens to be there) to help you measure your position on track.

Be sensible though, and do not use bits of paper, bits of old rubber or rocks, or even shadows, as there are very good reasons why these might not be in the same spot next time you come round! Always be vigilant – choose a marker and adjust your position from it as required, but do not forget what you are using and do not get carried away.

11. Blind Corners What happens when there are no visual keys though, such as on blind corners?

Blind corners represent an interesting challenge, but still conform to the overall rules for any given corner. It will still have all of the facets that any other corner will have, and the only difference may be that you cannot see some or all of the turn. Perhaps you are unable to see the turn-in point. Perhaps once you have turned you cannot see the apex or exit point.

Irrespective, and given that the corner is still definable by the various parts of a corner, the only fundamental difference may be that of confidence – we all like to know where we are going, and are much more comfortable when we can see our direction.

Where you come across a blind corner, the same rules of approach will also apply. Take it easy to start with and understand where the track goes and what sort of speed you can carry into and through the corner.

Always build up to, rather than attack, the corner – biting off a little more each time can make a much larger difference to your confidence, and

this will make you quicker, smoother and safer through the corner. It sounds more complicated than it really is, but try to visualize the corner and your route through it.

Perhaps the most important thing worth considering with blind corners, however, is that you potentially cannot see either into it, or the far side of it. Whether that be apex or exit, you should be very mindful of the closest marshal post to the entrance to that corner.

You need to know that the exit is clear. The marshal can see the other side of it, so he is the only person able to give you that information. Is he waving his yellow flag? If he is, slow right down! Ask yourself if you can stop safely in the length of tarmac that you can see. Your safety and that of any crashed driver(s) or any marshal(s) on track over the crest, or round the corner, depend on your vigilance.

12. Gear Selection Your gear selection is critical. In all stages of slowing down, cornering, and accelerating you should first and foremost (and this sounds obvious but still has the capacity to flummox experienced drivers) *know* what gear you are in. Do not just think that you know, and if you are in any doubt move your hand quickly to the gearlever and touch the top of it. Since, given your track position, revs and speed, you are unlikely to confuse second gear with fourth, or any other combination of gears on the same side of the gate, you should immediately be able to identify the gear that you are currently in, and from there you should be able to deduce whether or not that needs altering.

Never assume that your markers will be in the same place next time around. Since the last lap, someone has clipped the apex cone and flicked it into the infield. The driver appears to be using the end of the kerbing as his apex marker in this late apex corner, and a closer look confirms this as accurate, as it shows the orange paint locator there, where the cone would have been.

Remember to return your hand to the wheel quickly. (It is accepted that this will not work with sequential shifters, but in these cases hopefully the car has an indicator somewhere obvious that can be easily referred to.)

You should always *know* (not think that you know) when approaching a corner, braking zone or other such hazard (such as slow traffic, marshals' flags, and so on) which gear will be appropriate. A lot of this information may be derived from your

Even at the turn-in cone, you still cannot see through this blind corner. Take more care, visualize your line, be aware of the marshal post before, and then just follow the sequence.

49

previous lap and the information gathered from it.

We have already established that a neutral throttle is required before turn-in, so if you know that you require third gear for a given corner, then make sure that you have it engaged before the turn-in point – the gear should be in, the clutch should be up, the throttle should be neutral (or slightly positive if required) and the car should be stable.

If you are changing down a gear then the visual clues in front of you are likely to dictate whether or not you are going down one or two – there are very few circumstances where anything else would be appropriate. If you are changing down one, time it so that the car is running slowly enough to accept the gear – this means that you will have commenced braking and will be some way into this. If you are changing down two gears then you have two choices. You can break the change into two single gearchanges, or you can change the two gears at once by rolling the lever round the corner of the gate.

Only take this latter action if you are confident, particularly where you are relying on some engine braking for the next corner. (As an aside to this, it is rarely worth going round the gate to select third gear from fifth gear, as the risks of catching first gear, and consequently the risk of engine damage, are disproportionately high – this is definitely one to break into two individual shifts.)

When changing up, consider several things. First, listen to the engine, as you may not have time to glance at the rev counter each time a change is required. Get in tune with what the engine sounds like and this will help enormously.

Consider where you wish to change up – is it close to the rev limit, or are you using a lower self-imposed limit, or some other marker on your rev counter? Whichever it is, try to be consistent – the fewer things that you have to consider on an individual basis the better, as it will leave you with more time to get on with the job at hand.

Think about what you can see in front of you – for example, do not change up just for the sake of it, especially if it is obvious that you are likely to

have to change down again straight away. If there is another corner, an obstacle, marshal's flag or other such visual clue, hold the gear, but blend out of the throttle (essentially reducing acceleration so that speed becomes constant again) so that the engine is not straining if higher up in its rev range.

Whichever way you are changing, and particularly if you are changing two gears at once, always try to move the gearlever smoothly. There is no value in rushing and making a hash of it, and the smoother the movement on the lever, the more chance you have of getting it right first time. There may not be a second chance if you are approaching a corner where you are relying on engine retardation too. Moving the lever smoothly and positively also reduces the amount of strain you are putting on the mechanical parts that you cannot see (but can occasionally hear when you get it wrong!) The gearbox's life will be longer and happier if you take a little extra time.

In any event, make sure that you have time for your up- or downshift, and do so early if you might otherwise find yourself doing it mid-corner, for example, or some other inconvenient (or distracting) time. Finally, if you do make a hash of a gearshift, try to always go back to the gear that you have just come from, rather than the one that you were going to, and then reassess your position and requirements.

13. Commitment This looks like a strange heading, but it is very important that through each of the sections described above, in addition to our watchword 'smoothness', there is one other common thread, and that is your commitment to what you are doing. There are a couple of ways to approach this.

First, whilst off track, you could play the given scenario through in your head, so that when you arrive at a corner, need to change gear, brake, or carry out any other track action, you know what is required, how to achieve it, and that you are able to commit strongly to that action. You may have seen the action happening in your head, so you apply the brake positively, turn in with one smooth positive action, change gear with a firm hand knowing which gear you are selecting and when it has engaged.

However, this is not quite as straightforward as it sounds, as you are trying to process a lot of information at any given time when out on the track. Allow yourself time to build up on any given day, and you will find that in chasing consistency, as discussed elsewhere, the ability to be positive when you get to the appropriate marker should follow. Each of the previous laps offers additional and very useful reference points too, all adding to your familiarity with the circuit and offering a small confidence booster.

The second method of ensuring that you act positively when making decisions and committing them to action is to allow yourself a little more time when you are required to make some input. If you are on unfamiliar territory with a new track, brake a little earlier, select your gear a little earlier.

Ensure that you have these actions completed with the car just waiting for you to turn in, giving yourself a little extra time to consider your visual clues and then react to them positively. This applies to any action that you need to take, and not just those used here as examples.

Take a little time when sitting in your car in the paddock before venturing trackward to think about how you wish to approach your session, and be positive about your actions.

You should never approach the track without being positive. Being vague about the corner, the brakes, the steering and your interaction with these things amongst others, leads to indecision. If you find yourself still deciding what you should be doing after you have started doing it, you are taking away your ability to process those things that you should now be reacting to, or your ability to process effectively what comes next.

You are already at risk of error. If you find yourself with indecision worries when at the track, talk to an instructor who will be able to get to the bottom of what is causing these problems to occur. Once ironed out, though, you will find a greater purpose and dedication to your day, hopefully offering you more enjoyment from the whole track experience. Be decisive.

14. Conclusion That breaks down 'the corner', the most important single aspect of your lap. The various components of each corner will be the same in principle for each corner on each track, and now you should be familiar with these elements, and you should know how to prepare yourself for, and react to, the approach to each corner.

Flow

We have seen that the components of the cornering sequence look rather like a list of things to do. It would be relatively easy to simply 'join the dots' of the sequence for each lap.

Taken as a list of things to do, however, the steps of the cornering sequence could make for jerky progress as you finish one and move on to the next. With practice and confidence come the skills to link the steps quickly, efficiently and yet still smoothly, to make it all flow.

Transition

Transition is, in this context at least, defined as the linking of one step in the sequence to the next, (say after braking, coming off the brake pedal and back on the throttle). 'Smooth' is again one of the key-words here, although we could also add 'pace'.

Although there should be far more focus on making the transition between steps smooth, the faster you can get it done the faster you can get on with the next part of your manoeuvre, corner or lap.

Practice and skill should ensure more feel in both hands and feet (and backside), more confidence in your commitment, and better timing as you move from element to element. Then you will blur the edges of the various steps as you build your skill set and become more proficient.

6 Improving Your Lap

In seeking to improve your lap, you can experiment with a huge number of variables, and these will largely depend on the amount of processing power you feel that you can commit to each aspect of your on-track performance on the day.

- Perhaps the easiest items to quantify change in are the concepts of braking a little later and more firmly, and accelerating a bit earlier and more firmly, into and out of corners.

- Try adjusting your line a little to see if there is an improvement with a slightly earlier or later apex, or try experimenting with getting the car stable fractionally earlier to see if you can carry more mid-corner speed.
- Try altering your gear selection for corners where you could conceivably use either, say, second or third, to see if the alternative works better.
- Try not holding on to steering lock on the exit of the corner to see if it enables you to

In this complex sequence, you could experiment with your exit from this lefthander; perhaps it will help with the tight right-hander that follows?

use more throttle sooner.

- Experiment with your line in complex -corners to see if there is a better compromise in exiting the first corner earlier or later, or entering the second one earlier or later.
- Try to understand more of what the car is telling you via the controls to see if you think that there is more or less grip available than you think that you are using. This is particularly true on damp or wet surfaces.
- Try to remove your focus from the cones laid out and see if you can function without these pointers. Make your own markers and then adjust from there if you feel able.

Try to only make small adjustments each time, however, so that you do not have to dramatically adjust any other aspects of your corner.

This list is not exhaustive and there are a vast number of ways to make improvements to your skill set, and your lap as a result. The instructor will be able to offer some sensible targets for you to aim for if you enlist his help, and these could be derived from any of the above improvements, or from many others.

However, when attempting to improve your lap, do not take on anything that you cannot handle. It is all very well adopting good practice in braking a little later, getting into the throttle progressively but that little bit earlier, taking the corner at a few revs more, but if you cannot see a way of improving what you are already doing in whatever respect, then do not make the attempt.

This is how people come to grief and although there will always be some way to make a small improvement, if it is not obvious then do not worry. The instructor is best placed to see what you are doing and to see where you can add to your skill set – take a break and find him, and ask for some help.

If working on a particular facet is not for you on a given day, why not simply aim for consistency, and rather than improving by adding to any given component of your driving, improve instead by achieving overall consistency. Once you have done this, you may find that another improvement you were looking for presents itself to you in any event. Never push beyond what you feel comfortable with though – it is a recipe for disaster, and there is always next time.

If none of these approaches sound right for any part of your day, then why not take the pressure off yourself, and go out and have a few laps simply for the enjoyment of having a few laps? Enjoy the speed, the thrill, enjoy whatever facets you have learned today, and go home with a big grin on your face.

Finally, remember that you will never stop learning at the track – there is always something that even experienced drivers take home from each outing. It might be a very small thing, and it might be something much larger that you have been looking for for a while, but there is always something to learn. Do not believe anyone who says that they have learned nothing about themselves, their car or trackcraft.

FOLLOWING ANOTHER CAR

When you are following someone else round the track, whether by chance or by judgement, pay particular attention to your own actions. Obviously you should be aware of the other car, but only where it may interfere with your own progress. At all other times, try to look straight through it as though it were not there.

The reason for this may not be obvious, but following someone else can lead to you becoming pre-occupied with them, and you can mimic mistakes that they make almost without even knowing it. Going too deep into a corner, missing an apex, even having an incident – these are possible outcomes.

It really is not that obvious but ask any seasoned track-dayer or an instructor and they will all admit, if they are being honest, to having had a moment where they took their eye off the ball and became 'hypnotized' by the car in front.

OVERTAKING

You need to be very aware of the rules for overtaking, so listen very carefully to the briefing given in the morning as there are a number of circuits and organizers out there and you should not assume that their rules are the same as those at the last briefing you attended.

If you are the slower car, we have discussed the fact that you should be aware of those catching up with you, but that you should not let this distract you from your own job in portions of the track where there is an overtaking veto. This means that you should pay particular attention to the briefing to establish where these areas are.

Once you know that you are going to have to facilitate someone's passing you, make sure that you make the appropriate physical signal, whether that be pointing over your head, or indicating, and then move your car clearly to the appropriate side of the track, adjusting your speed if necessary.

Do not back right out of the throttle if you do not have to, and if the following car clearly has the measure of your own speed, you may quite reasonably elect not to back out of the throttle at all. Common sense and intelligent processing of what you see behind you are the keys here.

When moving the car, make sure that you do so in a positive but unhurried manner and that you do not de-stabilize it in your haste to be polite. Before you get to the point of making the adjustment though, and before any of the actual passing manoeuvre happens, remember that the most important thing that you can do is to 'do your own thing'.

Do not alter line, brake or speed up – do exactly what you would do if being followed by nothing, as this is what the driver behind will be expecting you to do. *Do*, however, expect the unexpected, such as those drivers who will pass you very close by, pull out at the last minute, pull in before they really have space to do so, and who may be quick on the straight, but who may completely spoil your approach to the next corner. Be patient and do not lose concentration – by the next straight they will hopefully be gone and you can get back to your own driving.

If you are overtaking, make sure that you consider where you are likely to catch up with the

Overtaking is generally allowed on the straights only. Although not quite straight, the track behind the car here is an allowed spot at Anglesey.

car that is in front of you. If you have the option to follow the car for a while as you catch up then take note of how the driver is behaving and what the likely outcome will be when you do finally catch up.

You will likely as not be disallowed from aggressive use of your lights, so make sure that if you do intend to give a light signal that you do so about (and no less than) 100m from the slower car. There is a far greater chance of someone seeing your lights from there, and a far greater chance that they will react well to the signal.

Make sure that you have received a very clear signal from the slower driver; whatever signals were deemed appropriate in your morning briefing are fine, but be prepared for the odd driver who has a different method of signalling their approval of your passing, even if they probably should not be employing it here.

It is also worth waiting for them to move their car to the appropriate side of the tarmac before making your move, as with some cars the indicators are easily knocked on and not easily noticed if you are concentrating hard. Be sure that you have their consent though. Once that has been given, make sure that you get the job done efficiently and quickly, where your performance differential allows. Equally, before consent is offered, make sure that you know what you will have to do to get past and on your way. Consider your gear selection if they have slowed you down on the way out of a corner, for example.

Consider dropping back a little to ensure that you are nowhere near them coming out of a corner and that you have good visibility through and around them, and make sure that if you have to go the 'long way round' you do not cut them up, or pull in earlier than you should, particularly in wet weather where their visibility could be adversely affected.

When following someone closely, be ready for consent to be offered at any time and know what you need to do when it is, but do not be annoyed or distracted if it is not this time.

A small acknowledgement of the courtesy of consent is nice, but do not do so where you would prejudice your control of your car, and do not reach for hazard warning light switches and the like in your enthusiasm for being polite. Raise a hand if you must, but all things considered you have far better things to be using your processing time on.

It is very conceivable that in passing or being passed you may find yourself off your chosen line and some compromise may be required as you approach the next corner. You may care to refer back to the corner 'entry' and 'exit' sections (*see* Chapter 5, sections 4 and 8 of Cornering), as amongst other aspects, you may need to adjust your speed, your steering input may have to be greater, and your gear selection may even have to change.

Remember that each incidence of this happening will be different, so you do need to be vigilant where it happens. Try to focus on your own lap rather than the other car in the equation. On any track day where there are no rules given for overtaking, the first consideration is to be **very** careful when either passing or being passed.

GRAVEL TRAPS

You will be hoping that this next section is of no relevance to your day, but you should make sure that you have understood it nevertheless, and *before* you get onto the track – it could save you a deal of heartache (and money).

Gravel traps, such as they are, are designed to stop cars hitting barriers, and they are very good at doing so. They will generally allow you to haul your car out again undamaged provided that you follow one simple rule. If you have to hit a gravel trap, *hit it straight on.*

Hitting them at an angle, particularly when you are carrying some speed, can (and will) tip your car onto its roof. Set this in your mind beforehand, and make a clear decision that should you ever stray from the blacktop and into the gravel, that you will not attempt to maintain steering in the hope of coming out of the other side and rejoining the circuit with a good story to tell of an evening.

The arrow helps highlight the perfectly straight (but faint) tyre tracks, but the skid marks on the edge of the tarmac indicate that the driver, once out of luck, drove absolutely straight into the gravel.

Steer straight and let the car stop – it is far better to be towed out than lifted out.

There is the potential argument that the gravel trap may not have enough length to deal with your surfeit of speed – in this case, it may be potentially worthwhile attempting to steer if you are going to cause some damage anyway, but your level of risk aversion may decide that a front repair is better than a bodyshell – cars that have been upside down are rarely worth painting!

KERBS AND WHITE LINES

There is a temptation to be a racing driver at the track. However, a word of caution. There are kerbs that are designed to be run over, generally on the outside of the circuit, and there are some kerbs that are designed to deter you from using them. The aptly named 'saw tooth' kerbs are brutal, and will give your suspension a pounding, the like of which it will get nowhere else.

Unless you are prepared to break something, and generally speaking no one should be that driven, since lap times are unimportant at track days, stay off them. If in doubt over any given

Drive straight into gravel traps where possible! There was clearly no attempt to steer here – no stories to tell, no bills to pay either.

Two examples of kerbing – a smooth one that is designed to be used, an extension to the track surface, and…

…one that does not necessarily deter you from using it, but it is rougher and you will find less grip on it.

kerb, stay off it too – they are unlikely to assist with anything you do, save perhaps straightening your corner a fraction more, although they can perhaps act as a useful escape margin if you should find that you need a little more 'track'. They can cause instability, given that they are frequently not flat, so if you find yourself on one do be wary.

Kerbs are generally painted, so you should really be aiming to stay off all of them when the day is wet, as they will be far more slippery than the tarmac of the circuit. If you find yourself having to use a wet kerb be very careful about steering, braking and throttle inputs – keep everything very smooth and controlled and traverse the kerbing as straight as you can (*see* photo at top of page 58).

This may sound obvious, but white lines are also painted on to the surface of the circuit. Paint, generally, is fine when dry, but can be disproportionately slippery in the wet. Therefore, a good rule of thumb, particularly on quick wet corners, is to stay well clear of anything painted.

WET CIRCUIT

It goes without saying that on a wet circuit you will be travelling slower. There is generally a great deal less grip and therefore you should be even more sympathetic with your inputs to the car.

If you are smooth all the time then you will find that this helps in the wet conditions, given that you will have far less chance of upsetting the car with harsh or twitchy inputs on brake, steering and throttle. You should still be mindful of the fact that you may have a smaller margin of error on, for example, quicker corners.

When the track is wet, start even slower than you would normally and build up even more gradually allowing yourself time to take in the conditions, what the car feels like, and how comfortable and confident you are.

Wet conditions are great for learning about yourself and the car, and many drivers who approach a wet day dreading the slippery track and otherwise poor conditions, come away absolutely beaming as they have had more fun

This exit kerb is glassy with rain, and will be disproportionately slippy compared to tarmac – take this corner a little more conservatively and leave some margin in these conditions to avoid finding yourself having to rely on the kerbing for a little more space.

than they thought possible. Do not be intimidated by the dampness – enjoy the fact that it will add another string to your bow and put more skills in your track day cupboard.

A drying circuit requires care too – almost half of this track has dried yet the other side remains slippery.

Track lines can be different in the wet, but this is something for the very advanced. Ask the instructor for assistance if this is something that you think that you are ready for, but do not become pre-occupied. There are probably better things for you to be focusing on.

When the weather is inclement, be prepared for a request in the briefing that you drive with your headlamps on dipped beam for the duration of your session or track time. If you forget before leaving the assembly area or pit lane, you can be sure that the marshal stationed there will make some odd gestures to remind you before allowing you on to the track – check your lights as this is perhaps what they are requesting of you.

WHY DID THAT HAPPEN?

Even seasoned drivers come up against this dilemma from time to time, the only difference being that perhaps their experience may allow them greater insight into working it out.

Quite often on the track you will have a 'moment'. Something that did not happen before, when preceded by the same number and the same type of inputs. This can be confusing for the novice driver, although it can sometimes be equally puzzling for the experienced one too.

Take a break and a breath and try to think rationally about exactly what may have been different about that corner or that gearshift, that apex, braking zone, steering input or hesitation, whatever it was that caused the 'moment'.

Doubtless something was a little different; perhaps a few more revs into the braking zone, higher gear through the corner, accidental clip of the kerbing on the way through the apex, not allowing for a better exit from the previous corner when approaching the next braking zone, but generally somewhere along the way there will have been a reason for whatever happened.

The reason for establishing what happened is straightforward and important. If you did something different to the car then you can iron it out and make sure that it does not happen again. If the car is doing erratic things to you then you have a problem.

If you do not understand which of these it is, then how can you be sure that it will not happen again, get worse or even cause you to crash the car? Understanding what happened will help with your skills and it will help with your confidence levels on the day.

Do take that break and run it through in your head – do not go and try to recreate it, as that is just asking for trouble. If you cannot figure it out, then seek out the instructor and try to explain all of the things that were happening beforehand, such as revs, gear, track position and corner, and see if they can help. Their previous experience should have them asking you a few questions and offering some possible explanations, or perhaps just the one if the circumstances point to it.

Quite often, just in the process of thinking it through and chatting about the occurrence itself, they can prompt you to the answer. Then you can

Why did that happen? Left-hand wheels off the edge of the circuit in an attempt to get straighter across this blind chicane, perhaps?

get back and drive that bit of track with confidence, and perhaps a pointer as to what to do differently, or perhaps just what not to do.

Naturally, it is possible that you encountered debris (perhaps dust, gravel, mud, grass or bits of vehicle) on the circuit. If this is the case, you are likely to know what happened and why. Fluids on the circuit, however, are more difficult to spot, simply by their nature. Perhaps your car was more reluctant to turn, stop or accelerate – if you spot other vehicles having similar trouble this may reinforce your assumption of spillage. Be very cautious if you believe that you have encountered fluids.

These scenarios are slightly different from others, but perhaps there is something that you can learn from them anyway – perhaps just the sensation of the incident, and how to sort it out could be useful.

Conceivably you could be alerted to what the debris or fluids looked or felt like (remember your view angle can be very oblique particularly if you are seated quite low down) and what to look for in future. Try to find a positive in each scenario as it adds to your experience and confidence.

7 Ending the Day

COOL DOWN

At the end of each session, and particularly at the end of the last session of the day, you should always (and that means *always*) give the car a proper cool down lap. There are a couple of reasons for this, and a couple of good exercises that you can employ to ensure that you give the car the best cool down lap that it can get.

First of all you should remember that the likely result of your track endeavours are that the brakes are significantly hotter than they will ever get on the road. If you are able to, try not to touch the brakes for the complete lap – this has an added

Water Temp

On a cool down lap keep a weather eye on your coolant temperature gauge. Try to properly reduce temperatures to normal road levels if possible.

benefit of focusing you on the racing line and corner speed too. Try it next session.

Naturally, the engine will also be hot, and you want to select the highest gear that you can at any given point on the cool down lap to allow the car to get plenty of air through its radiator(s) and oil cooler(s) and so forth. If you have a manually switchable auxiliary fan you may find it helpful to run this on your cool down lap.

Both engine and brakes can suffer from heat soak (where the latent heat of engine or brakes literally 'soaks' into the surrounding components) when you stop the car in the paddock, and the following exercises minimize the effects of this happening.

First, *always* make sure that when you return to the paddock the car is parked in gear with the handbrake off to prevent serious heat soak in the rear brakes.

Second, it is good practice to roll the car forward (or backward) a small distance every couple of minutes right after your session to prevent corresponding problems with the front brakes too. You can always open the bonnet to help with cooling the engine if you think that your car will benefit from this.

Be vigilant with your mirrors on this lap, particularly on an open-pit day, as there may be other drivers on circuit still at full track speed – be careful not to get in their way as you 'cool down'.

The reason that this cooling down is especially important on the last session of the day is self-evident. You have to drive home afterwards. Do not attempt any last minute heroics, no last minute chasing the dream lap. Make sure that from the second you note the chequered flag on the end of that last session (or the self-imposed end of any other session if you are taking a break – *never ever*

Arm up, signal left, the circuit here has additional width to ensure that you stay safe when entering the pit-lane. Ensure that you listen very carefully to the briefing for requirements but above all make sure that you signal your intentions early enough to allow other cars to notice you!

ENJOY YOUR DAY

Detailed earlier in *The Glovebox Guide* was the fact that people attend track days for very many reasons. Some are motivated to drive their car to the absolute limit of both its and their own abilities, some like the challenge of driving faster in the comparative safety of the race-track, and some are exploring the performance of their car. A lot of people may simply be there to have fun.

Driving quickly and safely is enjoyable, driving the track is enjoyable, getting something from your performance car that you cannot get on the road is enjoyable, and there is something innately enjoyable about taking your daily-drive car to the track and doing things with it that you just cannot do anywhere else.

Whatever your motivation for being there, do have some fun. If you have achieved what you set out to achieve then relax, enjoy the rest of the day and leave with a silly grin on your face. If you came to simply get a silly grin on your face then good on you. Remember, whatever your motivation, have fun.

RULE NUMBER ONE – YOUR MANTRA

do 'just one more lap') you focus on getting all of the temperatures down.

And this means your own too, so that you can park the car in the paddock, enjoy the last chat with your friends, and still saddle up for the ride home happy that the car is in one piece, you are in one bit, that you have learned from the day, and have really enjoyed the fun aspects of track driving today.

Above all else – remember the one and only rule that you should have at the back of your mind all day long, from the minute you leave your house, until you have driven your last track minute. There is only one rule. Rule number one – always drive your car home.

There is no more sage advice – do everything in your power to follow it. Enjoy the track!

Appendix I

Booking Confirmation Sample

Thank you for your booking, details as follows.

Date	18 March (confirmed)
Location	Matuide Park (National Circuit Layout)
Session	Intermediate (10:20 and hourly thereafter)
Sign on	from 7:30am
Briefing	9:40am (mandatory attendance)
Scrutineering	from 7:45am
Noise testing	from 7:45am
Circuit opens	10:00am to 1:00pm and 2:00pm to 5:00pm

Arrive 7am and get tyres changed

This is a non-competitive event, run in accordance with ATDO rules. Slick tyres, competition cars and competition licence holders will not be permitted.
There will be no timing allowed, and anyone caught timing via whatever means will have their wristbands removed and will take no further part in the day.
The noise limit on track today will be 98dB and this will be rigorously policed.

Thanks,

Track Booking Team.

Other useful information – helmets are mandatory and are available to hire at £10 for the day (booking required); fuel is not available at the circuit (nearest fuel station with Super Unleaded is 4.7 miles); catering facilities will be open all day from 7:00am.

Remember fuel canister – no fuel at circuit

Appendix II

Flags

In the briefing you will almost certainly come across some advice as to the motorsport system of flags, and you will be seeing some of these flags at almost every track day you attend.

They are the best way that the circuit marshals have of communicating with you whilst you are on track, and you should know what each flag's message is.

YELLOW FLAG

This flag held stationary is a caution flag, and means that you are approaching an incident of

some sort. You should be mindful of that fact, and in cases where you cannot see the incident, you should reduce your speed so that you are able to take appropriate action when you do see it.

The yellow flag waved is still a caution flag, but one of greater urgency. You are potentially almost on top of the incident and where you still cannot see it you should adjust your speed to the point where you have enough time to avoid the incident.

Whilst you are under yellow flag conditions you are not permitted to overtake.

GREEN FLAG

The green flag is an advisory flag, and it has two distinct uses. Following the yellow flag incident above, the green flag means that you are clear

of the danger zone and can resume normal track speed where it is safe to do so. You will be allowed to overtake slower vehicles again.

Additionally, it can be used on the opening laps of any session to indicate to you that the track is clear of hazard and is ready to be used today. You may find, for example, that the marshals all hang out a green flag when you are out behind that pace car at the start of the day.

Caution is warranted here though as you may not be allowed to overtake under these circumstances – listen carefully to the briefing for this advice.

Red and Yellow Striped Flag

This flag is a caution flag, and where you see it you would be advised to tread cautiously for the first lap or so after it is held out. It is indicating a slippery surface to you.

This could be as the result of fluid spillage, a quick shower of rain, gravel or dirt on the track surface or one of many other things. Be careful when you see this flag and do not attack the track until you have assessed the available grip.

Chequered Flag

No, regrettably, you have not won a prize! The chequered flag will be used to indicate the end of your session. It is your cue to do a proper cooling down lap (see 'Cool Down' section) as you have one lap before you park your car up again.

If you are on an 'open pit' day you may conceivably only see this flag once at the end of the day, although it may be thrown out at lunchtime where there is a lunch break.

You may be under yellow flag conditions when the chequered flag has been shown (listen carefully in the briefing for this advice) and this means that you should slow down and there will be no overtaking allowed either.

BLACK FLAG

The black flag is shown to you specifically rather than the other flags which are general advice. If you are shown the black flag you are required to come off the circuit the following lap, and speak to either a) the marshal who showed you the flag, or b) any other official of the organizer.

You should treat the following lap as a cool down lap (see 'Cool Down' section), and then report to the appropriate individual.

There are two reasons that the black flag may be shown to you. The first is mechanical failure or other issue with your car that you may not be aware of. Do have a look in your mirrors just in case you have not noticed that you are trailing smoke, for example.

If this is the case find a marshal's post and stop as close to the post but as far from the circuit as you can in case you are on fire or you are dropping fluids. If not, proceed slowly.

The second reason that you may be shown the black flag is as a result of some driving standards infringement. It is important that you understand what is alleged so that you can address it, as it may be something that you are not aware of. It may also be that if you do it again, your day may be prematurely terminated.

RED FLAG

This flag is an important one.

Your approach to it will be as if you have just seen the chequered flag, but slowing *right* down, and on this occasion you need to remember that overtaking is not permitted. You are required to return to the paddock or assembly area (this will

likely be indicated to you). The red flag means that the session has been stopped.

It effectively means that the track is closed and this could be as the result of a serious incident or spillage, very seriously inclement weather, or perhaps some other event that the organizer deems dangerous enough.

Note that some circuits have the capacity to turn on gantry lights and repeater lights round the circuit to assist in advising you of a red flag situation. Pay particular attention at the start/finish line for such lights, and watch for these elsewhere round the circuit (see photos overleaf).

BLUE FLAG

This one is rarely seen at a track day.

The blue flag held stationary is a caution flag. It means that there is another vehicle following you close by. You should be aware of this, and with a nod to the overtaking consent rules of the day, you should be thinking about how and where you intend to allow this other vehicle to pass.

Given the overtaking consent rules of the day, you should never see the blue flag waved. Here, it is also a caution flag, but of greater urgency too. The reason that you should never see it, is that it means that there is a vehicle overtaking you or attempting to overtake you, and you should be

Coming onto this start/finish straight, there is no way that you should be able to miss the gantry of red lights advising that the track has been closed and the session stopped. Proceed with great caution for one more lap and park up as directed. Remember that there is no overtaking.

Some circuits have repeater lights to assist with marshals' flag signals. Here the repeater box is clearly visible on top of the marshals' hut, and is just above your eyeline as you begin to make your turn.

aware of that given the rules regarding overtaking today.

WHITE FLAG

Another one that is rarely, if ever, seen at a track day.

Where you come across it though, you should be very acutely aware of its meaning. This flag is indicating that there is a slow-moving vehicle on the circuit. This may be another car with issues, a recovery vehicle, but the reason that you should be very cautious when (or if) you see this flag is that it may be an ambulance.

Be very vigilant!

Appendix III

Harnesses

A lot of people will never have come across harnesses before. A logical extension of the seatbelt idea, harnesses are generally secured from four points, or sometimes five.

Instead of having a 'lap and diagonal' strap configuration as a seatbelt does, harnesses have two lap straps that join together in the middle, and straps for each shoulder too. If there is a fifth one this is usually a crotch strap.

There are different types of fastenings holding these various straps together, but first to be connected and tensioned in all cases are the lap straps. Ensure that you get your backside pushed firmly to the rear of the seat and sit back before starting. These should then be done up as tight as they possibly can, perhaps just bordering on the uncomfortable. Once you have done this you can tension the shoulder straps to ensure that you cannot move at all.

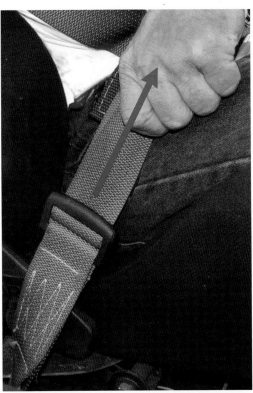

Tension the two lap straps using the adjusters at the sides. In this case pull upwards, although not all are the same.

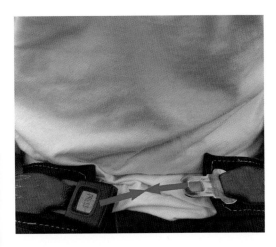

Fasten the lap straps first by simply connecting this seatbelt style fastener.

For those harnesses with four separate straps connecting to one central fastener, you can connect all four at once, but still tension the lap straps before the shoulder ones are tackled.

Unlike a seatbelt, a harness is designed to hold you firmly in your seat. Whilst having absolutely no movement might feel a little odd at first,

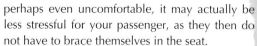

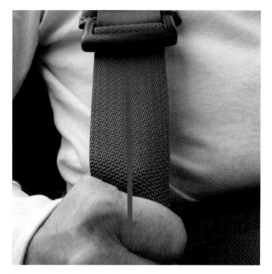

Shoulder straps next, and to adjust pull downwards until you are secured firmly. Slightly tighter than you might like is better, as harnesses can be really uncomfortable against braking forces if they are just slightly loose.

A one-word instruction manual – to get out of your harness in a hurry, it could not be simpler!

perhaps even uncomfortable, it may actually be less stressful for your passenger, as they then do not have to brace themselves in the seat.

Be familiar with how to release the harnesses in case you should have to do so in a hurry, and ensure that your passengers are familiar with this too

Appendix IV

Heel and Toe

This section is prefaced by a word of caution – if you are not familiar with this technique, *do not* choose a track day to try to understand it. (A straight road in a quiet industrial estate will serve you far better.)

With one of the main messages of track driving being that 'smooth' is better and faster, there are real benefits to be found in mastering the black art that is 'heel and toe'.

Described basically, this is a technique used to maintain stability when changing gear and slowing the car down. It involves flexing your right foot and ankle in order that both brake and throttle can be worked at the same time.

Normally under braking the right foot is generally placed squarely on to the brake pedal. When 'heel and toeing', the foot is rotated and placed on the pedal at an angle. The ball of the foot on the pedal still gives good contact and feel

for the amount of force being applied, but leaves the heel free in the air on the throttle side of the brake pedal.

Setting the manoeuvre up as above, when you come to declutch and change (down) the gear, you now have your heel free to blip the throttle to help match the engine revs to road speed in the new gear. Care must be taken not to apply more (or less) pressure to the brake pedal whilst flexing your foot – practice and skill will see you getting this right each time.

This gives at least two distinct advantages, the first being stability. The car will not lurch as the engine revs have to 'catch up' with the speed of the car, as in a more conventional downshift, nor will you encounter additional (perhaps unexpected) engine braking when the gear engages.

This gives benefits in the approach to the corner. This might mean that you could brake later, for

Foot centrally on brake pedal – conventional braking.

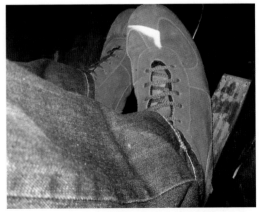

Pressure constant on brake – then press the right heel down for that quick blip of throttle, left foot down and up for clutch and hand for a gearshift. Practice makes perfect.

Practice the mechanics of heel and toe. Press the brake with the left and just flick the throttle with the right. Find a quiet road though!

Sometimes you may find that limited space means that using both sides of your right foot is the only way heel and toe can be achieved.

example, as you are not getting a large weight transfer close to your turn-in point. You may care to use the extra time to set up the car better for the corner if you are having difficulty here.

With the revs already matched to road speed, you should be able to set the throttle (and therefore target speed) earlier and quicker for the corner, giving potential advantages not only at turn-in, but throughout the cornering sequence too.

The second advantage is that the whole 'brake, downshift, back on the throttle and turn' process is condensed – having combined two of the elements you have saved some time. You may use the time to your advantage – or you may just have done a faster lap!

Practise, practise and practise though! Practice and feel will enable you to gauge how big a 'flick' on the throttle pedal you need to match revs perfectly. It will help you find that to master the technique the timing of the elements of the process needs to be very accurate. If you think that you are ready to explore this technique on the circuit, ask the instructor for some assistance once you have the basics – he should be able to observe and advise.

Do get the basics right first – go and find that bit of quiet road and just practise changing up and down the gears until you feel that you are getting it right. You could try just changing up and down without the brakes first of all, getting a feel for the blip of the throttle required. Add the brakes in when you are ready and try to get that smooth shift each time.

It should be noted that sometimes the pedal spacing and/or the size of shoe do not allow for the conventional 'heel' and 'toe' style. Sometimes you may find that using the left side of your foot for brake and then rolling your ankle to allow the right side of your foot to manipulate the throttle is the only way this can be achieved – there are a few other permutations but the outcome should be the same.

Also worth noting here is that, when practising this technique in that quiet industrial estate, it is more difficult to get it right with a lighter application of brake pedal pressure – naturally with track driving the idea is to minimize time on the brakes so do not worry too much if you find that you have to brake much harder to make the technique work for you!

Appendix V
Nürburgring

Winding its sinewy way through the Eiffel mountains in beautiful central Germany, the Nürburg ring is a staggering bit of tarmac. A Grand Prix venue until the seventies, and still an active race-track these days, on certain weekends of the year, you can turn up, pay your euros and take your own car round for a lap. Or two. Or three.

There are race-tracks and there are race-tracks, but the Nürburgring (the 'Ring) is like no other track you will have driven, or will ever drive.

Some of the most important words of advice regarding the 'Ring are words of caution. It is crucial to be aware that unless you are participating at a formally organized track day at the 'Ring, you are driving on an *open, speed-limitless, one-way, public* road. Inevitably, this means that you are sharing the road space with everyone else there, including tourists, locals, cars, vans and motorcycles, and even tourist coaches. This means that all of the rules of the German road system

The Nürburgring's toll barrier. Pay your euros, get your ticket and get ready for 100+ corners and tourists in Vectras!

No cones to help with entry, apex and exit. No run-off areas to bail you out of errors. Take your mettle and your concentration with you when you go to the 'Ring.

apply, including overtaking on the left only. You may be reported for doing otherwise, and this may lead to you being excluded for the balance of the day, or even prosecuted.

- Car to barrier contact will involve a chat with the roaming marshals who patrol the circuit constantly in appropriately marked vehicles, and will almost certainly involve you opening your wallet.
- Car to car (or worse still, car to bike) contact will inevitably lead to a chat with the police since, formally, you have had a crash on a public road.
- Dropping fluids knowingly may lead to prosecution, and if anyone is hurt as a result of a crash on your fluids, prosecution may get as serious as for manslaughter.
- There are charges for recovery, charges for clean up of the circuit, charges for repair of barriers or even closure of the circuit whilst any of these goes on, and your wallet will feel the sting.

All of this said, these measures are there for only one reason, and that is to temper anyone's zeal getting the better of their common sense.

The 'Ring is a public road, and whilst you can drive it at any speed that you feel comfortable with, you should always be mindful of the fact that there are well over 100 corners, cambers and gradients, and run-off areas that are measured in inches not feet! There are many, many surface changes, and the surface itself is rarely consistent in the same way that a UK race-track would be, there are vast tracts of the tarmac that sit under trees and do not dry quickly after rain, there are complex corners and very fast sections, very fast corners and blind corners. It is a huge challenge, it is easy to get 'lost', but there is also huge reward when things go right.

If you are determined to drive the track quickly, and there is no reason why you should not, you should be mindful of the fact that even experienced 'Ringers' will tell you that they are still learning, so once you have mastered the layout, to improve you should attempt to do so

Approaching at three-figure speeds, this very fast section has the blind crest in front followed by a very fast right-hander. Fantastic when it all flows!

gradually. Alternatively why not take advantage of some 'Ring guidance from one of the instructors located there, who are happy to help you out with corner, line, speed and all of the various factors that make up good, safe and fast 'Ring driving.

If you simply wish to say that you have driven it, it may be wiser to enjoy the experience than to attempt that high-speed lap. Certainly the place has an interesting atmosphere, great history, great scenery, great places to spectate (you can walk much of the perimeter and there are tremendous spectator areas set up for the various races that the circuit holds throughout the year) and locally there are many fantastic places to eat, drink and trade 'Ring stories.

The 'Ring is spectacular and quite unique, but be mindful of the challenge it offers. It would seem expedient at this point to make very specific reference to a couple of the sections from earlier on in the book too, particularly the section on recovery should you have a breakdown or incident here, and also perhaps to insurance. You should check your policies on both very carefully before going to ensure peace of mind.

If you do go, enjoy!

Glossary

Apex point: the apex point denotes the point on the inside of any curve where the racing line is closest to one side of the track. This is shown by the cone marked in the fourth diagram in the 'racing line' section, and in a 'conventional' corner would be almost half way round. There are variations to this, however – see 'Late apex' and 'Early apex'.

Bedding in: the process of settling new brake pads in. It involves increasing the heat that they are asked to deal with gradually, letting them reach full efficiency and creating a better contact patch with the brake disk.

Blend: this is often used in reference to throttle control, and simply means easing the throttle back a small amount to allow greater stability, a small reduction in speed where braking is not necessary or desired, or simply for a bit of confidence, perhaps in faster turns. Once you have 'blended' out of the throttle, typically it is then reapplied.

Boiled brakes: where the extra heat associated with track driving has transferred through the discs and pads to the brake fluid itself and literally boiled it. Since at this temperature, and frequently thereafter once cool again, the fluid becomes inefficient, your braking system becomes inefficient too.

Briefing: before taking to the track on each day you attend you will be expected to attend a briefing by the organizer. This is mandatory and you are likely to be issued with your track pass, wristband or windscreen sticker at this event to prove that you were there. The briefing is distilled essential information for the day and you should always listen carefully to the dos and don'ts for the event.

Camber: essentially the slope of the road surface from side to side. Camber can be positive – this would be a corner with the surface sloping into the corner, an element of 'banking' – which is beneficial to cornering as it holds the car into the apex. Camber can also be negative – a corner with the surface sloping away from the corner – which is detrimental to cornering as it throws the car out from the apex.

Chicane: a corner with a quick direction change, usually once left and then once right or the other way round. Can be fast or slow.

Confidence lift: notably found in fast corners, this is where you lift the throttle briefly and then reapply it before turn-in, simply to give the confidence of slowing down without actually braking. A psychological tool that helps you build to actually not lifting in this corner at all.

Corner radius: mathematically speaking, the radius of a corner is half of it's diameter, however, with a more colloquial reference in the track driving world, it is typically simplified to the tightness of the corner. A hair pin might be described as having a very 'tight' radius, whilst a fast open sweeper would be described as having a 'gentle' radius perhaps.

Early apex: this is where the apex point of the corner appears to be earlier than a 'conventional' apex; in other words before half way round the bend.

Fast sweeper: a fast corner that it is only really just a corner, with a (very) gentle corner angle or radius.

Feathering: this is the process of delicately adjusting the particular control you are using, but more commonly associated with throttle. 'Feathering the throttle' would involve gently reducing pressure on the throttle pedal to allow the car to maintain or retain stability and grip and to adjust the speed very subtly. Can also be used to refer to the removal of small amounts of rubber from the edge of a tyre's tread.

Hair pin: a corner with a very tight radius indeed, and aptly named as its profile looks like a hair pin. Can be left or right.

Heat soak: literally the process of heat 'soaking' into other components. Most commonly used in reference to brakes, where 'heat soak' means that when you park your car the heat that is already in discs and pads soaks into the surrounding components such as the brake callipers, brake fluid and even hubs and hub bearings. As this can have very detrimental effects, you should always try to minimize the likelihood of 'heat soak' in brakes, for example, by having a really good cool down lap.

Late apex: this is where the apex point of the corner appears to be later than a 'conventional' apex; more than half way round the bend.

Marshal: the men and women in charge of getting you safely to the end of your day. They wave flags, they man the pit-lane, they hold fire extinguishers and have first aid and mechanical qualifications. They are the cornerstone of British motorsport and a lot of it would not happen without them since a lot are volunteers.

Marshal posts: where you may expect to find marshals around the circuit. They may have formal huts, they may not, but they are strategically placed so that between them they have a complete view of the entire tarmac.

Modulating: this is the process of delicately adjusting the particular control you are using. For example modulating throttle pressure would involve gently adjusting pressure on the throttle pedal to allow the car to maintain or retain stability and grip and to adjust the speed very subtly, or perhaps increasing and reducing to effect grip

in low-grip situations. The same process can be applied to brake pressure where you may adjust pressure on the pedal very gently to help with a particular manoeuvre, or perhaps gently increase and reduce to prevent lock-up.

Moment: anything that wasn't scheduled in your lap. Could be a slide, a brake lock up, a close call with barrier, kerbing, grass, another vehicle etc. A colloquial term.

Noise testing: the mandatory (at some circuits) process of checking that your engine and exhaust noise falls within the limit for that circuit on that day. Method of testing will be specified, for example 'tested at two-thirds maximum revs from half a metre at forty-five degrees'. In this example, half a metre is the distance from your tailpipe(s) that the noise-testing device will be held, and it will be held at forty-five degrees to the outlet of that pipe.

Open pit: a track day run without sessions. Essentially, access to the track is unrestricted, hence 'open pit-lane', and you may come and go as you please, although the limit to the number of cars that the track is licensed for may still intervene in busier times.

Oversteer: where the car has become unstable and the rear is swinging away from the turn (so if the corner is to the right and the rear of the car has swung left), this is oversteer. To correct oversteer the steering has to be turned into the slide (i.e. for the example given turned to the left) whilst, preferably, all other inputs, such as throttle, remain the same. Rear wheel drive cars may correct themselves if throttle input is reduced, whilst in front driven cars more throttle can help drag the car straight again.

Progressive: a term often used with reference to handling, and meaning that the car, and particularly your tyres, do things in a controlled and gradual fashion. For example, say your car was reaching the limit of its grip on a given day, the grip would be lost gradually with the car starting to slide gradually, and not in a sudden moment with total grip loss.

Racing line: defined elsewhere in more detail in this guide, but essentially the smoothest and fastest, least bendy line round any given circuit.

Radius: mathematically speaking, the radius of a corner is half of its diameter, however, with a more colloquial reference in the track driving world, it is typically simplified to the tightness of the corner. A hair pin might be described as having a very 'tight' radius, whilst a fast open sweeper would be described as having an 'gentle' radius perhaps.

Save: this is the catching of anything defined as a 'moment' elsewhere in this glossary. If you are out of shape, whether on power or brakes, then gathering it all up and carrying on is a 'save'.

Scrutineering: the process whereby a circuit official or marshal scrutinizes your car to ensure compliance with the requirements of the day being run today. Can be to any level of scrutiny, but may include anything from the security of your video camera to the security of your battery, and anything in between.

Sessions: prescribed length track sessions, perhaps a set time, say quarter past the hour, and for fifteen minutes in every hour.

Slick: defined as being a tyre without tread at all, but can be found describing tyres that either have very little tread as a result of design or as a result of wear.

Stability: the effect noted when a minimum number of forces are being placed upon the car. Essentially, stability is when the car is not out of balance front-to-rear or side-to-side, and all the forces acting on the car are within the limit of forces that the tyres can cope with.

Steering lock: a term used to describe the amount of input or turn of the wheel used or needed to address the corner, manoeuvre or situation that you find yourself in.

Sweeper: a fast corner that it is only really just a corner, with a (very) gentle corner angle or radius.

Target speed: this is the speed that you wish to begin corner entry at.

Tramlining: where a car, usually with fatter tyres, follows undulations in the road surface, and impacts on your ability to steer the chosen path. If you are unsure as to how this feels, try driving in the inside lane of UK motorways where Heavy Goods Vehicles have worn 'ruts' – the car does not necessarily feel like it will go where you direct it.

Turn-in point: the point at which you make your initial turn into the forthcoming corner.

Understeer: where the car has attempted to carry on straight in spite of steering input, this is described as understeer. To remedy understeer less steering input is required to allow tyres to regain grip, and where the loss of grip was promoted by braking, less braking input would also assist.

Weight transfer: under braking (and acceleration) the front (or back) of your car squats closer to the road. This is the visible effect of weight transfer. Whilst there is no physical change to your car, the front gets 'heavier' under braking (the rear under acceleration), and this changes the balance and stability of the car. The more smoothly the weight transfers and this balance changes, the more stable the car is whilst it is unbalanced. The opposite is also true; when being rebalanced, the car will be more stable if the weight transfer is reversed smoothly. (Rearward weight transfer is another term for the effect found when accelerating or when releasing the brake.)

Circuit Listing and Useful Contacts

CIRCUITS OF THE UK

Anglesey Circuit
Bodorgan
Anglesey
LL62 5LP
Tel: 01407 811400/840253
www.angleseycircuit.com

Bedford Autodrome
Thurleigh Airfield
Thurleigh
Bedfordshire
MK44 2YP
Tel: 01234 332400
www.motorsportvision.co.uk

Brands Hatch Circuit
Fawkham
Longfield
Kent
DA3 8NG
Tel: 01474 872331
http://brandshatchcircuits.co.uk

Cadwell Park
Cadwell Park Circuit
Louth
Lincolnshire
LN11 9SE
Tel: 01507 343248
www.motorsportvision.co.uk

Castle Combe
Castle Combe Circuit
Chippenham
Wiltshire
SN14 7EY
Tel: 01249 782417
www.castlecombecircuit.co.uk

Croft
Croft Circuit
Croft on Tees
North Yorkshire
DL2 2PL
Tel: 01325 721815
www.croftcircuit.co.uk

Donington Park
Donington Park GP Circuit
Donington Park
Castle Donington
Derby, DE74 2RP
Tel: 01332 810048
www.donington-park.co.uk

Elvington
RAF Elvington
Elvington
Yorkshire
YO41 4AU

Goodwood
Goodwood Circuit
Goodwood
Chichester
PO18 0PH

Knockhill
Knockhill Racing Circuit
by Dunfermline
Fife
KY12 9TF
Tel: 01383 723337
www.knockhill.com

Llandow
Llandow Circuit
Marcross Farm
Marcross
Llantwit Major
CF61 1ZG
Tel: 01446 796460
www.llandow.com

Mallory Park
Mallory Park Circuit
Kirkby Mallory
Leicestershire
LE9 7QE
Tel: 01455 842931
www.mallorypark.co.uk

Mondello
Mondello Park
Donore
Naas
County Kildare
Ireland
Tel: 00 353 45 860 200
www.mondellopark.ie

Oulton Park
Oulton Park Circuit
Little Budworth
Tarporley
Cheshire
CW6 9BW
Tel: 01829 760301
www.motorsportvision.co.uk

Pembrey
Pembrey Circuit
Pembrey
Carmarthenshire
SA16 0HZ
Tel: 01554 891042
www.barc.net/venues/pembrey

Rockingham
Rockingham Motor Speedway
Mitchell Road
Corby
Northamptonshire
NN17 5AF
Tel: 01536 500500
www.rockingham.co.uk

Silverstone
Silverstone Circuit
Northamptonshire
NN12 8TN
Tel: 08704 588 333
www.silverstone.co.uk

Snetterton
Snetterton Circuit
Norwich
Norfolk
NR16 2JU
Tel: 01953 887303
www.motorsportvision.co.uk

Thruxton
Thruxton Motorsport Centre
Thruxton Circuit
Andover
Hampshire
SP11 8PW
Tel: 01264 882222
www.thruxtonracing.co.uk

TRACK DAY COMPANIES

Bookatrack   www.bookatrack.com/0870 744 1635
Circuit Days   www.circuitdays.co.uk/01302 743827
Easytrack   www.easytrack.co.uk/01469 560574
Goldtrack   www.goldtrack.co.uk/01327 361361
Heritage   www.heritagetrackdays.com/01508 536290
Javelin   www.javelintrackdays.co.uk/01469 560574
RMA   www.rmatrackdays.com/0845 260 4545

TRACK DAY LISTINGS

Openpitlane   www.openpitlane.co.uk
Hottrax   www.hottrax.co.uk
Trackdays.co.uk   www.trackdays.co.uk/0844 888 7700
UK Trackdays   www.uktrackdays.co.uk

NÜRBURGRING – THE NORDSCHLEIFE

Official Website   www.nuerburgring.de
Ben Lovejoy's UK Site   www.nurburgring.org.uk

DUNLOP CIRCUIT GUIDES

Picking up where the Autosport Circuit Guide left off, this publication has a corner-by-corner listing of every UK circuit. It breaks down the corner into what you can see, what you cannot see, what you need to know and what you need to be wary of. It offers advice on brake, turn-in and apex markers and position, along with cambers, bumps, ripples and general car positioning advice. There is a European circuit version, and a dedicated Nürburgring edition too.

2008 UK Circuit Guide   ISBN: 1-902204-19-0
2008 Euro Circuit Guide   ISBN: 1-902204-20-4
Official Website   www.circuitguides.com

Index